Fuel for Life

Abundant Living
through Daily Coaching

KIMBERLY ANN HOBBS

For information regarding special discounts for bulk purchases, please contact the publisher: LaBoo Publishing Enterprise, LLC

staff@laboopublishing.com
www.laboopublishing.com

Introduction

As you read this book, *Fuel for Life,* may you be blessed. May it extend to you the nourishment needed as you partner this book with God's Word by applying it daily to reach a fulfilling life of abundant living.

I asked God to breathe life into your soul while you're reading and to show you ways to achieve an abundant living lifestyle. God is in the process of educating each of us for His future service. Within the encouraging, fuel-charged pages of this book, you will see that God desires more for you than just "getting by." God wants to awaken your soul to His possibilities in your life by giving you food for thought each day and ways to structure truths into practice for your day-to-day living.

My ongoing prayer is that this book will be life-transforming for you just as it was for me while writing it. I pray it is the" fiery fuel" that keeps you "alive in Jesus" as you read the "charges" given over each day. May these soul-stirring nuggets of truth help you to understand God has YOU in mind for His purpose, and He desires for each of us to set a goal to have the kingdom lifestyle of abundant living while we are here on earth. Let it be not only for a single day but for a lifetime.

HOW THIS BOOK CAME TO BE

Through years of experiencing struggles, crooked paths, and painful consequences from the wrong choices in my past, I have chosen to resolve all to Jesus. As a result, my life has changed dramatically. My path is now clear and straight. I walk in freedom and abundant living as I joyfully serve my Lord. I have many life lessons to share with the wisdom God speaks of in James 1:5…Godly wisdom (I prayed years asking for James 1:5) and forward growth in my life's walk. Through it all and over time, God gave me a powerful story of redemption. I knew in my heart that one day, God would provide me with an opportunity to share my journey, my story through leadership coupled with writing, which would help others develop their own story and overcome hurdles in their personal lives. It has been a work in progress with God's direction.

I prayed that through encouraging others to step toward the abundant living lifestyle He has so graciously given to me, I would find my valuable purpose through serving Him, and I did.

Years ago, I started writing a book, which I had put on hold. That book brought healing to my soul. I know God will use it one day. I am still in the waiting period with it, but it has been sealed for a purpose. My desire is to help others in areas where God has shown me grace, mercy, forgiveness, and hope for my future.

While putting down the storybook of my life several years ago, I started a coaching group on Facebook. I began writing again but in a different way. My writing turned to daily life coaching through what I was personally conquering in my life with God's help. This amazing gift God gave me grew into a daily coaching challenge for others in three aspects of life: faith, food, and finance. People gravitated towards the helpful information the coaching provided, and God was touching lives. Soon, all the life-giving coaching God allowed me to share consumed my heart, mainly within the faith aspect of coaching through my life experiences.

God continued to speak truth into my heart through years of writing for various purposes and groups, along with coaching friends, loved ones, and countless other people who God brought into my life over time. Leadership and writing allowed me to understand that God has given me a special gift, the ability to encourage others in ways that move them to better choices and allows them life-altering results. It became evident that God was moving people. He was using my coaching skills and encouragement for others to accomplish this, and it began to spread like fire. My desire to help others overcome challenges in their lives grew with enthusiasm as did my desire to do it more for my Savior and King.

As I had contemplated writing *Fuel for Life*, I recall a moment I won't ever forget. Out of the blue, a prophesy was sent to me. I didn't know who wrote it, but I knew God had planned for it to reach me at just the right second so I would know it was from no one else but God Himself.

The timing couldn't be more miraculous. With all its POWERFUL words and knowing what I had just asked for in deep prayer to God, goosebumps covered my entire body as I read it.

I had prayed over *Fuel for Life,* asking God if I should continue writing this book. This prophesy came minutes later in a private message through Facebook by an unknown person, and it sealed what had been stirring in my soul: the desire to write a faith-based book solely for God and His purpose.

Within the words of this prophesy is my hope that you will hold on to this meaning for yourself and understand this word is meant for you, also, because you are about to read *Fuel for Life*. It's intertwined. Place yourself into this prophesy that is so fitting of what you will soon learn in the pages of *Fuel for Life*. I believe it's for you if you feel led to read the content of this book. The author is unknown to me, but my heart says they would give "ALL GLORY TO GOD" for these written words and what is received from them by the reader. It's my prayer that these words speak to your heart as they so POWERFULLY did mine.

THE PROPHESY

Dear Children of God,

This is a significant season. The battle has been intense because of the tremendous breakthroughs the Lord has for you. The battle has been intense because of the new chapter the Lord is opening in your life. It's not something to fear; it's something to rejoice in.

For the enemy has come against many of you time and time again to SIFT you, but the Lord is decreeing that He is now SHIFTING you. He is moving you. You are not going to remain in the same place.

The Lord is building momentum in your life, and He is moving you. He is changing circumstances, moving mountains, removing boulders, and making a way where there is no way.

The Lord is opening this new chapter in the book of destiny that He has written over your life, and things will NOT remain the same. I want you to hear this today. I felt it strongly on the heart of God for you. The enemy has told you many things for you will never change. That's a lie! The opposite is true! The Lord is SHIFTING and CHANGING things even if you don't see it yet. The Lord is making a way where there previously has been no way. Where those giants have been in your land for SO LONG—refusing to move and continuing to taunt, oppress, and torment, they are being driven out of your land by the hand of God. The Lord is moving powerfully within your life even if you don't see it yet. He is setting things up that are far beyond what you have imagined. (Ephesians 3:20)

In a vision, I saw the Lord opening the books of destiny over the children of God. Suddenly, as it opened, the wind of the Spirit began to blow strongly, and the pages were turning. *(Fuel for Life)* The pages filled with decrees, plans, and blueprints of God for His children. However, at the same time I could see the destiny that He had written for His precious ones, I suddenly had a strong sense of fire, the fire of battle and opposition. The atmosphere was full of this sense of "relentless battle" for so many children of God.

With tears in His eyes, His heart full of love, and compassion for His children, the Lord spoke so gently...

"Look at their faithfulness in the fire. Look how they have continued to stand and cry out to me in the midst of their pain and their torment. Look how they have remained devoted to me."

Suddenly, I began to see visions before my eyes of the many children of God pressing through the fire, standing, decreeing, holding His hand, looking to Him and offering Him a sacrifice of praise in the midst of the fire turned up seven times hotter. I could feel the heart of the Lord so intensely. He had seen. He had heard. He was moved.

His heart was moved. He was moved by the hearts of many of His children that had been through the fire yet remained in a place of intimacy and tenderness towards Him, continuing to trust even amid the most difficult of onslaughts. Their faithfulness and trust of the Lord rose to Him like a sweet-smelling fragrance, such beautiful worship to Him.

My eyes fell back upon the book, and I saw a new chapter open. Suddenly, the pages stopped turning.

AND NOW...

Where might God direct your life as you read through the daily coaching in this book? As your coach, my heart's desire is that God will show you what He's calling you to do for Him and the abundant living you can possess while doing this. There are daily challenges I encourage you to process and apply where needed.

The author of this prophesy is unknown to me, but I feel the message it has brought for all of us is for certain from God.

He has a purpose and a plan for your life, and as these pages turn, may you draw closer to both His purpose and His plan over your entire life and walk with Him while living in the abundant life in which He has intended for you to live.

Remember, He can do exceedingly, abundantly more than you can ever ask or imagine according to the POWER that is at work within you. Ephesians 3:20, if you allow Him to.

To God be all the glory within this book, forever.

Day 1

FIGHT TO FOCUS

If you're anything like me, it is very easy to become distracted these days. Our thoughts wander from what are we going to do with our day to what shall we eat. Then there's the constant interruption of our ringing phones and email alerts. The bottom line is we all experience distractions; our minds are being taken off what really matters.

What matters most to you? Take a moment to ponder that question. As a coach, I am encouraging you into abundant living. After all, that is why you're reading this book. I want to guide you to what God says matters most, which is our relationship with Him. We need to fight to focus on that.

God has called you to a purpose and plan in your life, but the forces of hell are trying to distract you from that course. They want to divide your heart, separate you, and pull you in different directions. If those forces distract you from what matters most, they can succeed in causing division, discouraging your soul, and disengaging your faith. The devil doesn't need to destroy you if he can distract you.

Diminish the distractions and fight to focus. If it's people who distract you from your focus, remember to walk with the wise, and you will become wise, as well. Walk with fools and become a fool. We need to do whatever it takes. Treat distractions like temptations. *Don't be fooled: "Bad company corrupts good morals."* (*New International Version*, 1 Corinthians 15:33) If you're not growing closer to God, treat the distraction like it is temptation.

Fight with everything to focus on importance. In Proverbs 4:25, Solomon says set your gaze on the path before you with fixed PURPOSE. Look straight ahead. Ignore life's distractions.

Remember, Peter began sinking in the water when he took his eyes off Jesus. Fix your focus. (Matthew 14: 22-33) Feel the joy of the Lord empowering you as you fight to focus on Him. Feel the happiness as you are propelled forward when you fight and focus on what's important. Your King is your prize; your destination is with Him. Listen to the voice of God. He is too good to waste on things that don't matter. Don't take your eyes off the prize. Your prize is your PURPOSE God has called you to.

You have multiple voices speaking toward you constantly. Listen to the simple voice of God. "*Whether you turn to the left or to the right, your ears will hear a voice behind you, saying, this is the way; walk in it.*" (*New International Version*, Isaiah 30:21) I love to use this verse whenever I can.

Fight to focus and hear God speak to you. Tune out the other things that distract. God can speak through His Word, Spirit, people, songs, and more.

Imagine the forces of hell pushing you to sell out to what doesn't matter, distracting you from what does. As your coach, I encourage you to call out to God to redirect you to the things that actually matter. Make a conscientious effort to try this today. Examine and filter your distractions. Focus your spare time on your "importance list".

God gave you gifts, a purpose, a way to make a difference in this world. You matter. Fight to focus and know nothing else matters but what matters most to God: YOU. Put everything down and focus your gaze on God. Hear the voice from heaven that says you did good. You'll hear it when you focus.

His master replied, "Well done, good and faithful servant! You have been faithful with a few things; I will put you in charge of many things." (*New International Version,* Matthew 25:21)

You can make a difference in this vast world if you understand you have a fixed purpose and God is calling you to it. However, you must "fight to focus" and push aside all the distractions that can interfere with your calling. I'm cheering you on to abundant life, but God is calling you to it. Don't ignore the call. Fight to Focus!

Day 2

TRAIN YOUR MIND

Our life is always moving in the direction of our strongest thoughts. If we can't control what we think, we won't be able to control what we do. Most of life's battles are won or lost in our minds.

Many of us have strongholds, which is a wrong thought pattern. We must be careful not to believe the enemy's lies. We need to remember God's truths. Fix your thoughts on what is true, noble, pure, and lovely. God says think on such things. (Philippians 4:6)

I know when I am going in a wrong direction with my thoughts. Because I have trained my mind, I am able to stop them. That is only by the POWER of God working in me.

We need to train our minds.

Write it. Think it. Confess it. Believe it. I encourage you to practice this daily.

You are free – and not a hostage – to your thoughts. You have the mind of God directing your thoughts. God is all about truth. God is truth. God says we have not been given a spirit of fear, but of power and of love and of a sound mind. (2 Timothy 1:7)

When those wrong thoughts rise in your mind, confess them immediately. God is faithful to forgive those thoughts and cleanse your mind.

One way we can do this is to meditate. What that means is to engage in mental exercise, focus one's thoughts. Try focusing on one verse each day. Meditate on the words of that verse or even just one sentence in that verse. Allow it to come active in your mind.

His Word directs your path. His Word is a lamp to your feet and a light to your path. (Psalm 119:105)

You are strong in Christ. You are free. You are a child of the Highest. You are a weapon of righteousness in a dark world. Write it. Think it. Confess it. Believe it. Your life has value.

Be fruitful in your thinking today.

Day 3

OPTIMISTIC OR PESSIMISTIC?

Each day when we open our eyes, we have a choice to either be positive or negative.

Do any of us think to focus on God's blessings and the wonderful possibilities of living life for him on each given day? Or do our thoughts immediately return to our troubles and what is far less than what God has for us?

Each day, I must conscientiously choose to be optimistic. Trust me, it's not always easy being positive, and I often succumb to the pressures surrounding me. My days end up wasted, and deep inside, I know it's the choice I made by my attitude.

I was reading in Philippians about the apostle Paul who, although physically imprisoned, chose to wake up spiritually free each day. He consistently chose to show gratitude over grumbling. He chose to be joyful over being depressed. He chose to trust God over doubting him.

There may have been a reason God kept Paul in prison. It is there that he wrote the letters which gave us lessons, encouragement, and warnings. Paul could have chosen to sit in prison and rot away in self-pity, depression, and pessimism. If he did, you and I would not have some of the most life-changing accounts of his life from which to learn.

What does God want to do in your life? Despite our "feelings", it should be our heart's desire to choose optimism and be used by God on any given day versus pessimism where we can be appalling to even ourselves. Think about this as it plays a pivotal role in the health of our body. Our minds are powerful creations.

Prayer can help with this. Pray often for your family and friends, which can affect your attitude. Pray for a thirst of knowing God deeper and that He would become a passion in your life.

Remember often and memorize this verse to help your view:

"Don't worry about anything, but in everything, through prayer and petition with thanksgiving, present your requests to God." (Christian Standard Bible, Philippians 4:6)

Today, let's all try to choose joy for our attitudes and our health, as well as the health of those surrounding us.

Day 4

DEPENDENCE

When we think of the word dependence, many of us may connect it with addiction. I think of a child clenching the side of its parent's clothing.

The exact definition of the word dependence is "the state of relying on or being controlled by someone or something else."

God says we need to live in dependence on Him. By doing so, we will enjoy an abundant life.

One way we can learn dependence on God is to appreciate the tough times because they will amplify your awareness of God's presence in your life. For example, a job we once dreaded can become a wealthy opportunity when we start to enjoy a "closeness" with our Savior.

When tired or weak, remember God is your energy and strength. Lean onto Him and find pleasure doing so, especially when you are lonely. It will allow you to draw closer to God and become dependent on him.

When around others, we often lose sight of God's presence. Fear of letting others down puts us in bondage to them. They can quickly become your primary focus. When you realize this, whisper God's name, and He will draw close to you. I do this often, and immediately it brings me close to God.

Tiny acts of trust bring God ever so close and in the front of your consciousness. That's where God belongs. When you find joy in your dependence on God, he can flow through you to others.

When you learn to allow God in your forefront, even around people, you will soon experience dependence on God and abundant living.

I looked up a verse on dependence – Jesus said, *"I am the vine; you are the branches."* (*New International Version*, John 15:5)

How much more can we glean from that scripture of being truly dependent to live? A branch cannot exist on its own; it must depend on the vine for all its needs.

Throughout the day today, practice drawing close to the one who created you. He's waiting for your dependence on Him.

Day 5

PEACE

On this day when you were able to open your eyes from sleeping and see what God has in store for you, I encourage you to look for peace. Often, I find my true inner peace when I look up to God.

Try not to dash about this day like all the other days, bolting like a racehorse suddenly released from the gates. I can identify with this because it describes me before I reclaimed my new routine. I'm hoping to encourage you to go about another approach to your day. Instead, try walking into your day with purpose. Allow God to direct your course one step at a time.

Open your eyes with gratitude. A grateful heart protects us from negative thinking. Thankfulness enables us to see abundance all around us.

God's love gives true inner peace. It fills all our space, time, and eternity.

Be on guard against self-pity. When you are weary or not feeling well, this can be the greatest trap you face. Be on guard and stay a safe distance from this pit. We can protect ourselves by fixing our eyes on God.

When sitting quietly, allow peace to settle over you. Feel God's loving presence. It is a rare treasure to find true inner peace.

One verse that can help to focus on this search for peace is – "*Thou wilt keep him in perfect peace, whose mind is stayed on thee: because he trusteth in thee.*" (*King James Version*, Isaiah 26:3)

This verse reminds us to keep our focus always on Him so that we may experience true inner peace and comfort.

I hope this gives you a thought for the rest of today and helps you focus on the peace that only God can provide. Dig deep inside your being and find the quiet love that God wants to blanket over you. May you find comfort, security, and His presence of perfect peace enveloping you as you move about throughout your day.

Day 6

DISCIPLINE

Discipline is something I've prayed over with intensity. In my past, I have had struggles with many forms of discipline. I'm not rebellious; I just don't like it.

When you think of discipline, what comes to mind?

I think of children who need discipline, feeling it may bring forward better behavioral qualities. Honestly, it's difficult to think of myself being disciplined as an adult. Am I alone with thinking this?

Often, this can be a result of pride. I don't want to think I've made a mistake, only to be corrected by someone else's view. But, how does God view this?

At the end of today's writing, I will share a portion of scripture that will explain God's view on discipline.

Maybe through a brief story, you will be able to relate in your own life how an act of discipline may help you.

One day, I received a phone call from someone who is very dear to me. The friend stated that my Facebook post had offended her. I have always been super cautious about what I post on social media, so her comment caught me off guard. My actions were not direct or deliberate to cause harm; it was quite the opposite. I thought my post was somewhat bizarre and even humorous. It drew an enormous amount of views and "likes" in just twelve hours. The post was a few photos of an extremely older man – who I did not know – walking on South Beach practically nude except for a shoestring and a patch. For whatever reasons, he appeared to want the attention drawn to himself, and in disbelief, I snapped some pictures as he passed by several times while parading the beach. I posted the few shots using the title "Only in South Beach".

It affected my friend in a way I never considered. Possibly others could have viewed it the way my friend did and just never said anything. From the hundreds of comments and "likes" my posts received, I thought everyone agreed with me. Unfortunately, my friend's view was one that never even entered my mind.

I was not alone in my reaction. Many who were on the beach were caught up in the oddity of what we saw. I just felt the desire to share it with everyone on my Facebook timeline, as well.

One thing I always do is pray before posting. However, this was one of the rare occasions when I did not. I was in such utter shock of what was in front of me at the moment that I posted without thinking it through.

I had no intention of causing any harm, but in another moment, I had to face looking at it from a different perspective. As I listened to my friend's view, I realized what I had done was wrong. After she explained how she viewed the post, I felt sad about my actions.

I could have easily justified the reason for my post, but I didn't. After all, I had the approval of so many others who responded to seeing the man the way I did.

God spoke to me in that moment of confrontation, though, and I immediately realized what I had overlooked before posting. Not wasting a second, I humbly expressed being sorry to my friend.

During that phone call, I received discipline. Not only was I ashamed, but I felt like I had shattered my example of leadership to that person who trusted me. I quickly tried to fix the situation by removing my post with the click of a button. Sure, I corrected the issue, and it was gone. However, my consequences were not.

For the next week, I beat myself up over and over about what I had done. The enemy wanted to take me out "in my mind" and not allow me to get beyond this. But, then, this verse spoke to me. *"As you endure this divine discipline, remember that God is treating you as his own children. Who ever heard of a child who is never disciplined by his father? If God doesn't discipline you as he does all his children, it means you are illegitimate and are not really his children at all."* (*New Living Translation*, Hebrews 12:7-8)

This truth came alive to me. I *AM* a child of God. So, of course, God will discipline me. *"...But God's discipline is always good for us, so that we may share in his holiness. No discipline is enjoyable while it is happening—it's painful! But afterward there will be a peaceful harvest of right living for those who are trained in this way."* (*New Living Translation*, Hebrews 12:10-11)

I had to endure the shame of what I did, but God loves me so much that he used this friend to gently explain to me in love the wrong of my actions. The incident I executed could have caused judgement and hurt to others who observed it. What if someone knew him or his parents saw the pictures I posted? Did I bring any harm to others? Even though I confessed it to God right away, I had to suffer the thoughts of concern. At that moment, I was being disciplined.

In the future, I will always remember that my life is being watched closely. This experience quickly turned into a wonderful lesson for me. I must always be accountable for how others might interpret my actions. I believe that through my friend, God disciplined me with love. I could have been prideful and rejected the call, but I did not. Instead, I humbly apologized and received God's discipline, which only makes me stronger each day. I'm grateful for the ways in which God deals with me. Knowing how much He loves me grows my love for Him.

"... The Lord disciplines those He loves." (*New International Version*, Proverbs 3:12)

God has brought me through this so I can continue to share in his holiness. (Hebrews 12:10)

As you try to identify with me – but in your individual situations of being disciplined, I pray we can all be thankful for the lessons we learn. Know that God loves you so much, he chooses to bring the wrong action to the surface somehow for the teaching of the lesson.

I look back and am so thankful this person felt led to call me. It's all in what God does to teach those He loves the most: His children. Are you His child? Be accepting of discipline; don't let pride stand in the way. It will bring health that is so much lighter and easier to carry than the burden of hiding from your mistakes.

WEAKNESS

Our health can flourish at times, but other times, all that seems to stand out is our weakness. I, for one, seem to be affected by my weakness and will sometime allow it to take me down.

Weakness tends to bring out the worst in me, and it can be painful. Can you relate? Why would God want us in a place where we focus on ourselves instead of the God-life that is in us?

We need to remember each day that God loves us, and He won't ever leave us.

You can feel like you're at your weakest moment, and often, it can be excruciating. But, don't give up. It may be a training process. This spiritual battle might prepare you and refine you for what's ahead.

The enemy tries to discourage you and make you weak by putting your flaws on display in front of you. But, thanks to God, He saves us through His amazing grace and the POWER of His undying love.

God promises to deliver provision to us through our weakness, and it seems to come J.I.T. – Just in Time!

A verse I love that I'd like you to hold tight to today is, "*My grace is sufficient for you, for my power is made perfect in weakness. Therefore, I will boast all the more gladly about my weaknesses, so that Christ's power may rest on me. That is why, for Christ's sake, I delight in weaknesses, in insults, in hardships, in persecutions, in difficulties. For when I am weak, then I am strong.* (*New International Version,* 2 Corinthians 12:9-10)

Remember, my friend, you don't have to be mighty in your physical body to be mighty in the battle each day.

You don't have to be physically fit to change the world. You only have to know the one who lives in you is far greater than the one who is in the world (1 John 4:4), and it is in Him that you will be used, despite your weaknesses to change the world.

I feel the need to include my life verse because it is so impactful. (Ephesians 3:20)

He wants to do exceedingly, abundantly above ALL we could ask or imagine, according to the POWER that's at work within us.

Remember, His power is stronger than your weakness. If He resides in you, these incredible things will happen. Not by your weaknesses but by His POWER!

Understand this and hold this close to your heart each day.

GENEROSITY

We have all heard the saying "It's better to give than to receive." But, did you know this saying breathes financial health into your life?

Generosity is the quality of being kind and generous.

Generosity often happens when a person is living from a condition of abundance and chooses to give. It can also be when the needs of others move a person. You can give out of your "surplus" or contribute even when you have very little, which is called compassion.

Both move God.

God is generous because he lives in a condition of abundance; His provisions can never be exhausted. God is also moved with compassion because he sees our need.

Do you ever question why so seldom we live generously? Maybe because we live in fear of what will happen if we exude generosity, or it may be because of our conditions of scarcity. Those are both normal feelings.

God shows us continuous generosity. We must learn from Him. Everything we receive from Him is a gift because it's free. We are breathing undeserved air, eating food grown from rain and sunshine – all gifts from Jesus. We have earned nothing, but God continues to give us all of these. God is not interested in what we can do for him. God is interested in something much more important than our good works.

God delights when we show generosity to others. He wants us to love others. What happens when we do that? Isn't more love poured out?

When we show generosity not only with our finances, time, talent, and compassion, our cup will overflow. (Psalm 23) It's not because of what we deserve when we give, but how God is always taking care of his loved ones no matter what we offer. We give in love because He first loved us.

Take an extra moment to read Psalm 23. It's not only for funerals or memorial services. It will help you understand our exceedingly generous God. If you read and meditate on this, your mind and body will soon become shaped by these words. I know this works. When I was a little girl, my grandmother allowed me to take a black magic marker and write the 23rd Psalm (in my third-grade handwriting, mistakes and all) on the back of her white bathroom door. Everyone who used that restroom had no choice but to sit and read that scripture that was from two feet away from their face. I think everyone in our family memorized that Psalm, as it remained intact for years and years.

Focus your attention and understand the impact generosity will have on your health.

Soon after you memorize this portion of scripture, I believe your heart can accept generosity, and you will begin to exude a generous spirit yourself, leading you on to healthier living.

"The Lord is my shepherd; I shall not want..." (*King James Version*, Psalm 23)

Day 9

MARGIN

This concept of margin is beneficial to me, as it gives me insight into my life. There have been books written about margin. Let me explain what margin is and why it's essential to our health.

Margin refers to the space on the edge of a page where there is no text. This book has margins at the top, bottom, and sides. If words stretched from the tippy top to the very bottom and all the way to the edges, there would be no margin.

I have to believe our lives are like this in many ways.

We add so much to our schedules that we have no "margin" or space for God, rest, family, fun, or health. The conditions of new millennial living devour our margin.

Example:

Margin-less is arriving thirty minutes late to your office because you were twenty minutes late to the babysitter because you were ten minutes late to drop the kids off at school because your car had no gas and you forgot to grab the credit card.

Margin is having money left at the end of the month and sanity left after the children go to school.

Margin-less is not having the time to watch a documentary on stress. Margin is having the ability to pause the documentary whenever needed and write down notes.

Can we all relate to this?

Dr. Richard Swenson wrote a book called *Margin*. He is a medical doctor who began noticing all sorts of health hazards caused by stress. He discovered stress came from overextension in our daily lives.

He started telling patients to slow down and eliminate unnecessary things from their everyday life.

Many of us compromise our health, family time, and relationship with God because we have no time. Isn't that three of our most precious resources?

We must work to create margin in our lives.

Get up ten minutes earlier to create a space for silence before starting your day.

Cut out unnecessary activities.

Scale back some of your commitments and decide the necessity of them.

Capture a moment of undivided attention with a friend instead of seeing them continually.

When we lack margin, we have stepped outside of our safe place. Be honest and be deliberate with your scheduling. Your spiritual health, physical health, and financial health all depend on it.

Day 10

NEGLECTING GOD

Many times, when I prepare to write, it's because of different convictions that prompt me. As I read my Bible today, I came across this verse and was convicted myself.

I read and considered this verse that stuck out to me, *"You expected much, but see, it turned out to be little. What you brought home, I blew away. Why?" declares the Lord Almighty. "Because of my house, which remains in ruin, while each of you is busy with your own house."* (*New International Version,* Haggai 1:9)

Instead of getting down to work and rebuilding their spiritual lives by rebuilding God's temple, Haggai said his people were more concerned with the condition of their own homes than time spent in communion with God.

To me, it's a warning to us not to be so concerned with outward appearances and selfish ambitions, but rather more concerned about the condition of our hearts and how we touch the heart of God. A self-check is always needed when I get into these readings. The good news is when something's broke, I fix it with the help of Jesus.

Haggai got upset with his people and told them to get their priorities straight! I, too, must remember to always place God first in my life. Any attempt at work I do without God's blessings and guidance will be unproductive. My material possessions will never provide me with the same satisfaction as God.

My reading friends, for your spiritual health, I encourage you not to allow ANYTHING to keep you from your daily prayer time with God. Do whatever is necessary to find time to be with God. He's our creator! Whatever we do in the spiritual – praise, worship, and prayer – lasts for eternity! Please try to incorporate at least one of these into your day today, if not all. Your life will be healthier because of it.

Day 11

DISPLEASING PRAYERS

Can anyone lend an ear on this topic? What is it?

I read a verse in Proverbs that prompted me to share. It made me stop and think, and in turn, I began to write.

"Anyone who turns his ear away from hearing the law- even his prayer is detestable." (*Christian Standard Bible,* Proverbs 28:9)

Lord, you have my attention. Can there be a time when my prayers don't please God?

Through reading scriptures, I've found that a consequence of our disobedience is that our prayers will go unanswered.

I looked up the word detestable; it means revolting, loathsome. I don't believe any of us would want God to view our prayers as being those things.

For me to grow in God, I have to keep asking Him to show me what He wants me to do. If I don't ask, I will not know. Even if I'm doing right, I must ask Him to show me where in my life I might be displeasing Him.

We can't receive all God has for us if we aren't living in obedience. How do we do this?

Jesus said if you want to enter life, obey the commandments. (Matthew 19:17) Walking in obedience doesn't just mean keeping God's commandments. It means listening to his specific instructions.

If God instructs me to rest and I don't, it's disobedience. If He's told you to stop doing a certain type of work and you don't, that's disobedience. If He's told us to stop looking at something tempting and we don't, that's disobedience. Whatever it is He asks us to do, remember that He does it for our good. Therefore, we need to try continuously to follow what He is telling us in His Word.

God's ways are always better than our methods, and staying in God's Word helps keep our paths clear and allows our prayers to be heard. It's important to me that I clear my conscience before I pray so that God hears my prayer. I feel confession to God should always be a part of our prayer life. I encourage you to make confessing a part of prayer in your time with God so you will be certain in your own heart that your prayers are heard.

Morning prayers are often a wonderful time to share gratitude with our Savior. I usually start by praising God for His creations and then name them. I thank Him for my blessings. There are so many I can't count them all. I follow this with heartfelt confession in areas God may be dealing with me.

Before we ask God what He can do for us, let's cleanse ourselves in His holy presence. This will bring confidence that we are forgiven and nothing ugly lingers between ourselves and our Creator. He is a forgiving God who loves us. He keeps no record of wrongs.

"He has removed our sins as far from us as the east is from the west." (*New Living Translation,* Psalm 103:12)

Rest in this today as you cleanse your hearts to pray to God.

SPIRITUALLY UNHEALTHY

Please understand that if you're feeling SPIRITUALLY defeated or unhealthy, you shouldn't throw in the towel. You still have hope.

If you're a believer, you have the Holy Spirit that resides in you. He will never leave you; God promises that. When we pray, we talk to God alone either out loud or silently. We may even pray along with others. Sometimes, words may not come because the pain might be too deep, the situation too confusing, or the fear too high. You may want to talk to God but don't know how.

Good news.

He promises that when we don't have words to speak, the Holy Spirit prays for us! He searches our hearts; He knows what's going on and HE intercedes. That means in times of grief and suffering, He knows what's going on and intercedes for us.

In times when we are uncertain and don't know the path ahead of us, He helps us to pray.

When we are afraid, we may not know who to turn to or trust, he helps us to pray.

In times when we are feeling overwhelmed or with a crushing weight of burden, He helps us to pray.

If you are feeling spiritually discouraged and unhealthy, the Holy Spirit is there helping you.

"In the same way, the Spirit helps us in our weakness. We do not know what we ought to pray for, but the Spirit himself intercedes for us through wordless groans." (*New International Version,* Romans 8:26)

I don't know about you, but that sure comforts me when I'm not feeling at my peak. God loves us so much He gave us that Comforter when we sometimes don't even realize we rely on Him! Wow, what LOVE!

As simple as this is, we tend to complicate it.

If life is overwhelming you at this moment, drop your cares into the lap of the one who loves you most. The simple word "help" is sometimes all that's needed. The Holy Spirit is already interceding on your behalf. Face today knowing you are not alone.

Day 13

FAITH/SIGHT

In my coaching when I start new with someone in their journey, I ask a lot of questions. I'm opening today with a question. How do you view victory and success?

I used to associate victory with success, not to fall or stumble or make mistakes. When I felt successful in my strength, I often forgot about God. I'd go on my way thinking I did it on my own. It could've been the smallest accomplishment, yet not acknowledging God in it only brought the buildup of pride in my life over time.

Later years – through problems and failures, weaknesses and neediness, I learned lessons and that God is the one on who I need to rely.

I realized true dependence is not just asking God to bless what I have already decided to do. It's coming to Him with an open heart and mind and asking Him to put his desires for my life inside me. At first, it was scary because I didn't feel I had control over the situations I once had. It was a different mindset for me.

I had to realize God is in control and achieving a goal is always in His ultimate hands. I, myself, cannot achieve such a goal.

Our journeys begin when we rely on God. It's a faith walk for sure. One step at a time. It's not a path of constant success but multiple failures. I've realized my best growth spurts come after my worst failures. Can you relate? I am blessed when I depend on God and not myself.

I encourage you to deepen your dependence on God and not yourself.

When I started my health journey, I gave it entirely to God, every day asking him for help. Guess what? Each day got easier. Before long, it became a new way of living for me.

I hope I can positively encourage you when it comes to your health. I only try to inspire coming from a place of past experiences that God has shown me the "good" in. It is for that reason I feel I do well with it.

"We live by faith, not by sight." (*New International Version*, 2 Corinthians 5:7)

I encourage each of you to allow God to have control of your situations by your faith in His desire for your life and try not to walk in only what you see in front of you. Life becomes a faith journey. May your day today be blessed, dear friends.

Day 14

STRENGTH

Have you ever needed an extraordinary measure of ability to handle an extreme situation or problem? Simply put, have you ever needed great strength?

I have, and I've even reached out to some of my friends for that help.

Sometimes we look at our situations and wonder how we are ever going to make it through. It could be a task that seems beyond reach, the sudden death of someone we love, a divorce, a chronic illness, a child raging out of control. Sometimes, we feel it's beyond our ability to cope.

As I read in Ephesians, God gave Paul the great inner strength of his unlimited resources. This encourages my soul.

No matter what darkest pit you must climb out of or highest hurdle you have to jump, God will wrap his love around you, covering and protecting you as you face it head-on.

No matter how great the storm is in your life right now, God's love is so powerful that it can give you the strength and ability to overcome any situation. Remember, it's not our strength; the strength comes from God. But, please, don't hesitate to ask Him for it.

"It is God who arms me with strength." (*New International Version,* 2 Samuel 22:33)

"God is our refuge and strength..." (English Standard Version, Psalm 46:1)

Please don't pause when you're out of strength. Go to God when you need it most. He tells us over and over in his Word.

"The Lord is my strength and my song." (New King James Version, Exodus 15:2)

Consistently praying is where I am now. Can I ask you where you might be?

I often have to encourage myself, remembering to ask God for strength. Try not to accomplish any difficult task in your own strength. Remember, God is our strength.

In the day ahead, whenever you feel difficulties moving forward, take it to the One who holds all your strength. Let Him be the POWER that gets you through the day.

Day 15

LISTEN

When we are given a direction to honor the word "listen", it's not complicated. We have a choice of what we accept in our minds and what we don't. We hear many different things swarming around us regarding health. What we should do and what we shouldn't do. Ugh! It can get overwhelming.

"Therefore this is what the Lord God Almighty, the God of Israel, says, 'Listen!'" (*New International Version,* Jeremiah 35:17)

We need to be diligent in monitoring what we allow into our minds when it comes to health and nutrition. The information we see on TV, the magazines we read on health, the books we read, and the people we talk to – everything begins in the mind. Filling your mind with thoughts that lead you to peace and blessings is better than thoughts that will lead you to fear, depleting you and making you feel empty, confused, or anxious. People use all kinds of extreme measures to get you to listen to them or follow them for advice.

Don't allow people to fill your head with their propaganda on how to live. Stop, be still for a moment, and "listen" to what God is telling you to do. Don't live with confusion. Ask God to give you clarity and knowledge of who or what information to trust. Ask Him to give you ears to hear His voice. Ask Him to make you a good listener. In time, I promise you will find yourself discerning all the information that is surrounding you, especially in the area of health these days. I know because it happened to me. God will make you a good listener if you ask. Listen for that voice.

"Whether you turn to the right or to the left, your ears will hear a voice behind you, saying, This is the way; walk in it." (New International Version, Isaiah 30:21)

Day 16

LIFE IS NO ACCIDENT

God knows everything about us. To me, it's such a comfort knowing my creator is always watching me. He knows my thoughts even before I think them. He knows yours, too. He knows your actions from the time you get up in the morning until the moment you go to bed. Even when you fall into a sound sleep, God is watching over you. Don't just take my word for it. Read it for yourself.

"You have searched me, LORD, AND YOU KNOW ME. YOU KNOW WHEN I SIT AND WHEN I RISE; YOU PERCEIVE MY THOUGHTS FROM AFAR. YOU DISCERN MY GOING OUT AND MY LYING DOWN; YOU ARE FAMILIAR WITH ALL MY WAYS. Before a word is on my tongue you, LORD, KNOW IT COMPLETELY." (New International Version, Psalm 139:1-4)

God is everywhere around us. There isn't anywhere we can go that God isn't there, too. That is a comforting fact to me, and I hope it is to you, as well. He is with you on your mountain top highs and your valley lows.

You may struggle with the way you look, and sometimes you may not feel too good. You may even feel like you're a mistake, but you are not! God formed you and loved you while you were inside your mother. Your life is not an accident, my friend. You have a purpose, which was established before you were born. We need to do the best we can do physically to protect our health and His purpose for us.

Healthy foods and thoughts will do our bodies good. God performed a miracle when He created you. Please believe your purpose is important, and you need to be healthy to fulfill God's plan for your life. Praise God every day that He knows and loves everything about you and wants you to be that healthy person.

I am praying over you as you take to heart the words on this page, my dear reader friend.

NEW HEART

Do the temptations of the world shatter your thinking or draw you away from focusing on God? This question hits hard for me because I always seem to have a distraction in my face in some form or another.

There is an old hymn I remember singing years ago that goes, "Prone to wander, Lord, I feel it. Prone to leave the God I love." We seem to drift away with our hearts and our emotions, which can deceive us into thinking something else is better than what God has planned for us.

"The heart is deceitful above all things, and desperately wicked; Who can know it?" (New King James Version, Jeremiah 17:9)

I believe there is One who can know our broken hearts and give us an undivided heart, a new heart. What does that mean for us? It means if we give control of our hearts to Him, He will renew us from the inside out.

If you think you can't give up that destructive habit, uncontrolled addiction, inappropriate thoughts, or the wrong relationships, then seek God. Chances are you can't do it on your own. Cry for His help. Ask Him for a new heart. God loves when we ask Him.

God will also remove our hearts of stone. Have you ever heard that?

"I will give them an undivided heart and put a new spirit in them; I will remove from them their heart of stone and give them a heart of flesh." (*New International Version,* Ezekiel 11:19)

Have you experienced pain and trauma that you told yourself you'd never allow to hurt you again? My answer is yes. Has your warm heart for things of the Lord ever become cold and distant? Mine has and still does from time to time. I choose not to allow these actions to continue; I can recognize it quite quickly and deal with it. When we invite God's spirit to live in us, He gives us a fire in our hearts that can't be put out. He nudges us when we need to listen.

Ask God to ignite this fire in you and burn away all the hardness. Ask Him for a new heart filled with love.

I feel the ultimate challenge for our heart health is to fix our eyes on Jesus no matter what is going on around us. When He is your focus, you will view circumstances from His perspective, and your heart will become new every day.

PLEASE go into your day today with the God who loves you held deep within your new heart. Look for spiritual health to revive itself in you.

Day 18

GOD'S PRESENCE

Every step of our journey through life can be a step of faith when you view it this way. I have found that by taking baby steps first, they become easier, and before you know it, you are almost walking with ease into situations you may have never dreamed possible. Giant steps can sometimes be difficult for us as we trudge through valleys of death and fear; steps of faith become harder during these times. Let's examine some reasons why.

As we are all different children in God's eyes, it's not for any of us to judge each other's "faith walk" or the "presence of God" in one another's lives. Some may hesitate at things they face or tremble in fear when facing a situation. Where those steps may be easier for you or me to take, others may not see it as such. When it comes down to it, sooner or later there will be things we cannot do alone. Every now and again, I catch myself and need to stop impressions of knowledge of my own accord or faking strength to endure difficult situations and humble myself to the One who never leaves my side. That is difficult to do, and it's called faith.

God has prepared a path for me, for you, for each of us. It's our choice to follow or not follow, to have faith and remain in God's presence or do it on our own. We need to be active in this world. This is true, yet one step removed from it and abiding in God's presence. I believe this is where we will find continued peace and safety. Remembering to stay in the presence of God who loves you most proves beneficial. I looked up the word presence in the Bible and found this verse, which I'd like to share with you. My hope is it brings you reassurances for this day as it has brought to me.

"In the shelter of your presence you hide them from all human intrigues; you keep them safe in your dwelling from accusing tongues." (New International Version, Psalm 31:20)

This truly brings me comfort along with peace and safety, and I pray it does the same for you and your spiritual health and well-being. No tongue can harm you when you are safe in the dwelling of our Savior. May you find comfort in His dwelling place throughout your journey of today.

Day 19

PREPARATION

"Prepare your work outside; get everything ready for yourself in the field, and after that build your house." (*English Standard Version,* Proverbs 24:27)

Half the battle is knowing what to do before you execute it. Set yourself up for success, not to fail.

Prepare for the day that stretches before you. Know what your day will contain exactly instead of only having a vague idea about it. It's like reading a map; you must know your destination before you can read the map to get there.

I pray about each day ahead of me. Then, I set my mind to follow that prayer, and throughout the day, I look specifically for those subjects I prayed over to be accomplished.

I have a few tips I can recommend. My example will be preparing for my physical health each day. My physical health improved when I started juicing. There are steps I take to prepare myself for the task. Yours may be completely different. Your preparation may not involve food. What might it be today?

As a coach, I'm going to share a routine I do that may help you.

First, give your entire task (or job) over to God. Ask for His help and direction with it. I am a huge proponent of this surrendering. I can't do anything with God's excellence by trying to do it alone. It may sound petty, but if I want true spiritual success within my task – and I always do, it must be done with God by my side.

The second step is to rid yourself of temptations that may bring about failure. I purge my home of all toxic foods and temptations. Therefore, I can't be lured to indulge in my favorite "guilty pleasures" if they aren't inside a cupboard or the refrigerator. Other tasks may call for ridding an area of tempting magazines, ones that can cause overspending or increase desires that are unhealthy. It could be throwing away stockpiles of unused clutter in an office to ensure clarity and cleanliness.

Third, if cost is involved in your task, establish a budget that will work for you and your family. Incorporate that into what you desire to accomplish. Knowledge of and preparation for the specific task ahead of time allows one to spend less money. It's a proven fact.

Make a list. For me, it may be the types of juices I desire to drink in a week; I'll need specific ingredients for that juice. To others, it could be something they are preparing to do outside of the home or business depending on whatever the task is. It may require writing down specific steps to follow. In the end, it saves time and money.

Lists are extremely helpful. Did you know writing things down engages our brains and many times allows us to remember something even if it's not directly in front of us? Our mind takes a photograph of it.

Prepare. For me, meal prepping helps me out when I have little or no time on some days. I keep something healthy around so that I'm not tempted to grab unhealthy foods when I'm hungry. For you, preparation may involve gathering extra material so you can save time and money by not having to run out to go to a store in the middle of a project. It could mean cleaning up your yard while the sun is shining versus waiting until the last minute when there's a downpour and guests are coming for a barbeque that afternoon.

In my case of juicing, I like to make extra juice in advance when I have adequate time versus frustrating myself when I'm rushing. Remember, feeling rushed can lead to tendencies of "giving up" on the tasks we set out to accomplish. Again, set yourself up to succeed, not fail.

My example can be used for any preparation. It pays to prepare ahead of time.

Again, *"Prepare your work outside; get everything ready for yourself in the field, and after that build your house."* (*New International Version,* Proverbs 24:27)

If you do this with God's help, He may not show you what's ahead, but He will equip you for the journey if you are efficient in your preparation. By staying in constant communication with God throughout each day, His presence will be the best road map for your success in accomplishing your task. May you have an organized, wonderful day.

Day 20

ARMOR

Do you ever feel like you are getting armed for battle and may be faced with mounting challenges when you awake for the day? I can feel this way, especially when I start a new routine that takes me out of my comfort zone. For example, when I start a cleanse – whether it be spiritual, food, juice, or just life, I tend to get uncomfortable. Why does this happen? To me, anytime I try to do something good, there is an opposition lurking on every shelf in the form of food or temptations in every corner that mess me up.

Good news!

Scripture tells us we are all in a spiritual battle. I am not alone on this, and neither are you. Be on guard constantly because there are spiritual forces of evil that are trying to defeat you. Those forces are trying to ruin your great intentions to be healthy in whatever area you may be choosing.

God says in His word that we should put on the full armor of God so you can take your stand against the devil's schemes. *"Put on the full armor of God, so that you can take your stand against the devil's schemes. And pray in the spirit on all occasions with all kinds of prayers and requests. With this in mind, be alert and always keep on praying for all the Lord's people.* (*New International Version,* Ephesians 6:11,18)

From the moment that we become believers and align ourselves with what God's word tells us regarding our faith, food, finances, and all the other areas of life, the enemy of our soul wages wars against us. But, know that with God's help and by calling on His name, you can overcome this!

Whatever your issue is, PUT ON YOUR ARMOR, as God describes in Ephesians 6:11-18.

"[11]Put on the full armor of God, so that you can take your stand against the devil's schemes. [12]For our struggle is not against flesh and blood, but against the rulers, against the authorities, against the powers of this dark world and against the spiritual forces of evil in the heavenly realms. [13]Therefore put on the full armor of God, so that when the day of evil comes, you may be able to stand your ground, and after you have done everything, to stand. [14]Stand firm then, with the belt of truth buckled around your waist, with the breastplate of righteousness in place, [15]and with your feet fitted with the readiness that comes from the gospel of peace. [16]In addition to all this, take up the shield of faith, with which you can extinguish all the flaming arrows of the evil one. [17]Take the helmet of salvation and the sword of the Spirit, which is the word of God.

[18]And pray in the Spirit on all occasions with all kinds of prayers and requests. With this in mind, be alert and always keep on praying for all the Lord's people." (*New International Version,* Ephesians 6:11-18)

It is the way we access that power and the protection God's word tells us. We need to be conscientious of this daily. It will give us knowledge, instruction, and ever-increasing faith.

Put on the full Armor of God and pray. I warn you that one can't face these battles alone; we must ask God to help us daily.

I couldn't have completed sixty days of drinking only vegetable juice to change my health with my own willpower completely. I asked God daily, hourly, sometimes minute by minute to get me through it...and He did! I am so grateful for that health change, and I want the best for each of you whatever challenge you may face in all areas of your health. Faith health, Food health, and Financial health. May you examine your battle today with God's help and armor up with His advice.

Please put on your Armor of God before committing to your challenges solo. Each day try to remind yourself of this necessity. I fail miserably at this and try to remind myself each time I face my battles. God is with me when I put on my armor, and I feel strong, empowered, and ready to face my day! He will be with you, as well, when you prepare for battle.

As you read this right now and prepare to face your day, please know I've already prayed for you!

Day 21

FORGIVENESS

There are times in our lives where this word can weigh heavily on our hearts. There may even be times we don't care to think about this word at all. We want it far from our minds.

Going into our day, we could be thinking about that certain someone who wronged us in a hurtful way, or possibly we possess the need to forgive ourselves in our relationship between ourselves and God.

To change our behavior in these times of need, three steps need to be taken, which God allows us to do.

The first step is to confess, admitting what we did.

Everyone makes mistakes. Unfortunately, in the times that we live in today, many people can't admit they've done something wrong. It is sad but true. God says all we must do is acknowledge the sin, confess it, and He will forgive us and make us pure.

Confessing comes first in admitting to ourselves, then God, and then maybe the one or ones we have hurt. We need to own up to our wrongdoing. It can be extremely difficult for some but well worth doing. It cleanses your heart by releasing that burden of guilt, thus allowing God's total forgiveness to take place.

The second step is repentance, being sorry for what we've done and turning away from the offense, heading in the opposite direction and not wanting to do it again. True repentance is being so sorry before God that you won't ever wish to let Him down again by repeating the offense.

Thirdly is asking for forgiveness so we can be cleansed and released from consequences associated with what we've done.

God wants us to live free of guilt. He wants us to live in complete forgiveness so we can find that total restoration in our lives that makes us feel complete again.

"If we confess our sins, he is faithful and just and will forgive us our sins and purify us from all unrighteousness." (*New International Version*, 1 John 1:9)

Don't allow anguish to overcome you today because you haven't experienced the true word forgiveness in your heart and life. Allow God's mercy to cover the offense that may be clouding your thoughts. Feel the freedom that you will experience when this happens. The true release that comes from forgiveness is yours for the receiving when you follow these steps before God.

Day 22

PRAYER GROWS LOVE

It is such a powerful thing when we pray for one another. Every time I pray for someone, I feel more connected to them. I feel my heart going out to that person, even if I'm praying for someone I don't know. Do you experience that? I believe it's because God gives you and I a "heart" for who we pray for.

Many of us say, "I'll pray for you" or "my prayers are with you", but do you remember to pray? We must be careful when we say those words. If we carelessly say them and don't follow through, it could end up being a lie.

Praying is a good thing and does our hearts good. Even praying for our enemies softens our hearts and opens the door to which God can hear our prayers and change the hearts of others. When I'm angry with someone, the last thing I feel like doing is praying, but if I focus – conscientiously making myself pray – walls come down, and I start to forgive. I always feel better about it afterward.

How about praying for someone else like intercessory prayer? It not only influences situations and other people, but it changes us in the process. While writing this, I'm thinking of many people I choose to pray for daily. Difficult people in my life, people who hurt me that

I may not necessarily "want" to pray for, and the list goes on. Can you relate? Let's keep asking God to help us pray for them versus ignoring the "prompting" we receive when we think of those people. When we do this, He works love into our hearts for them, which will ultimately be our biggest blessing, my friend.

"And in their prayers for you their hearts will go out to you, because of the surpassing grace God has given you." (*New International Version*, 2 Corinthians 9:14)

If we read this verse a few times and ponder it, I believe God will bring people to your mind that need your prayers. He will also bring you some beautiful blessings in the process.

I encourage you to step out on faith and pray for that one difficult person in your life today. You can do this!

Day 23

HURT/HEALTH
Part 1 of 2

Many days I find myself waking only to realize some recent or past hurt is still troubling me. What do I do? How can any of us find health amidst the hurt in our daily lives? We are thrown curve balls all too often, which seem to carry tremendous pain when they hit us head-on. How do we cope with these to protect our health?

If you have troubles, let me help you with a few reasons why being in God's word can improve your health in regards to your hurts. Regularly implementing this into my life eases my pain and brings about heart health.

God's word can bring wisdom, and as wisdom grows in you with knowledge of God's word, it helps you through your hurts.

"The law of the Lord is perfect, refreshing the soul. The statutes of the Lord are trustworthy, making wise the simple." (New International Version, Psalm 19:7)

Singing this Psalm out loud as a teen, I never understood the impact it would one day have on my life walk until now. It allows me to seek out God.

Another way to steer clear of hurt is to know where you are going. You can't see the future, but God's word will guide you.

"Direct my footsteps according to your word; let no sin rule over me." (*New International Version*, Psalm 119:133)

This verse shows us that we can't choose our steps any longer, Lord, take us where you want us to go. Release our past mistakes and gently guide us forward in your Word.

We must try to live a life of purity and holiness in order to enjoy more of the Lord's presence in our lives. We need to stay cleansed in God's word.

"How can a young man keep his way pure? By guarding it according to your word." (*English Standard Version*, Psalm 119:9)

By application, this will alleviate much hurt that we all too often bring upon ourselves, by not living in a pure and holy way of our actions.

If we don't understand God's law, how can we obey it to prevent some of our hurts from happening?

"Teach me, O Lord, to follow your decrees, then I will keep them to the end. Give me understanding, and I will keep your law and obey it with all my heart. Direct me in the path of your commands, for there I find delight." (*New King James Version*, Psalm 119:33-35)

I do not feel you can be free of hurt without the word of God in your heart. Joy can soon replace sorrow.

"The precepts of the Lord are right, giving joy to the heart. The commands of the Lord are radiant, giving light to the eyes." (*New International Version,* Psalm 19:8)

The definition of the word precept is a commandment or authoritative rule for action. So, God is telling us by obeying his words, joy will be restored over the hurt.

My prayer is that today this portion has given you food for thought. Tomorrow, I will share a few more ways to overcome hurt for your body's health.

Day 24

HURT/HEALTH
Part 2 of 2

As I encouraged you yesterday, you can overcome hurts by drowning yourself in God's Word. I can honestly say I've restored my health to a safe level by implementing some of these new (but old) ways of handling hurts.

When hurting, we need to look into growing more rooted in our faith. We can't grow in faith without reading or hearing the word of God. Listening to my audio Bible each day is a terrific help.

"Consequently, faith comes from hearing the message, and the message is heard through the word about Christ." – (New International Version, Romans 10:17)

We honestly will not know how to free ourselves of hurt unless we study God's word to find out.

"...If you hold to my teaching, you are really my disciples. Then you will know the truth, and the truth will set you free." (New International Version, John 8:31-32)

One thing I've learned is I am not experiencing true peace when I hurt. How do I get that peace? God gives it to me when the world can't, but I must find it in His Word.

"Great peace have those who love your law, and nothing can make them stumble." (*New International Version*, Psalm 119:165)

Everything has become so relative today. How can we know for sure what is right and wrong without God's word? I believe many of our hurts come from our choices; some good and some not so good. God has offered true forgiveness to get beyond our hurt and on to better health. He wants us to know His Word so deeply that we carry it wherever we go and use it to make proper choices for our lives.

"I have hidden your word in my heart that I might not sin against you." (*New International Version*, Psalm 119:11)

Many of the Psalms I read bring healing to my hurts. I find many of these verses in Psalms 119. I believe entirely that when you can rise above your present hurt with God's word in your heart, your health will follow with a glowing joy of restoration. Again, my prayer is that as your coach, these truths that help me will also help encourage you to welcome joy over sorrow in your daily life that's worth living.

Day 25

OUR HEARTS

How much do we consider the health of our hearts? I think about this often since heart issues run on both sides of my family tree.

However, the heart health issues I am speaking of today are our inner hearts.

"But the Lord said to Samuel, 'Do not consider his appearance or his height, for I have rejected him. The Lord does not look at the things people look at. People look at the outward appearance, but the Lord looks at the heart." (*New International Version*, 1 Samuel 16:7)

Isn't it comforting to know that God does not judge us in the same way other people judge us, or even in the harsh way we sometimes judge ourselves? God is concerned with what is inside our hearts. God doesn't place value on our outward looks or where we rank on social media, our financial status, or any other external things the world may consider important.

As I listened to my Bible app this morning, God said David was a man after God's own heart. His social status within his family was so low that he wasn't even called in from the fields to meet with Samuel. But David was God's choice to become king over Israel, and from his family line, we'd see a savior that God would provide to us! God didn't see David the way his own family saw him.

Sometimes others don't see you or me the way God sees us. God is always looking at our heart's attitude. I examine my heart as often as I think about it, which is almost daily. Are my motives right? Is God able to use my heart to help others? I, for one, know if God can use a young shepherd like David, he can use any of us in a big way, also.

We need to make our hearts available to God's POWER to see what amazing things he can and will do through us.

As I love to do throughout my coaching, I must share my life verse yet again. Hope you'll take the time to look it up in different versions. Today's version is NIV.

"Now to him who is able to do immeasurably more than all we ask or imagine, according to his power that is at work within us." (New International Version, Ephesians 3:20)

Day 26

HEALTH/HEALING

Taking care of our bodies is something we should do. When we ask God to heal us, it's something He does. Body care and healing are two different things.

God knows our imperfections. That's why he sent Jesus to be our healer. God gives us our bodies and wants us to live in balance, taking care of our bodies and not abusing them in any way. After all, our bodies are the temple of His Holy Spirit.

I hear many people say my body belongs to me, and therefore, I can do with it whatever makes me feel good. Caring for our body is not something we can do successfully without God.

Many people think if they don't take care of their body, God will still heal them if they get sick. This way of thinking is dangerous. Our attitude toward this kind of living will hurt us!

We sabotage our life by not doing what is best for our bodies and our health. Ask God to help you resist what is bad for you, and be disciplined enough to do what is good for your body; I can't stress this enough. We all understand that healthy eating takes discipline. Ask God to help you with self-discipline. If you're a person where

God's Holy Spirit dwells, you need to pay attention to your health! God loves you and values you, but He wants you to love yourself and value yourself enough to take good care of your body.

Ask yourself questions about your health. Is this beneficial for your body? Will this cause harm to your organs, like your heart, blood, brain? We all know what we shouldn't eat, habits we should break, and exercises we should do!

Sometimes sickness can still occur even after all the effort we put towards taking proper care of our bodies. How much easier will it be to go to our Healer and ask him for help when we know we've done EVERYTHING we possibly can to help ourselves be healthier? Please ponder the question I just asked.

Lord, I pray that in your presence my friends will find health and healing. Let them know they can reach out and touch you, and in turn be touched by you. This is my prayer today, Lord.

Amen.

$\mathcal{D}ay$ 27

SLEEP
Part 1 of 2

Do you know the reason many of us can't seem to function properly is because of exhaustion? We are living beyond our means, both financially and physically. As a result, we are neglecting something our bodies desperately need. Sleep!

Studies have shown the average person needs approximately 8 hours of sleep to maintain health. Failure to do this results in damage to our physical health, loss of energy, and decreased productivity.

Do you realize our sleep deprivation often hurts those around us? I know for a fact when I don't get enough rest, I am irritated and unable to focus. Usually, lack of sleep also affects how I look physically, which gives me a reason to try to hide from the world. It may not be true, but I act upon my feelings all too often. Who has that time to waste anymore?

I read somewhere that in the 1850s, the average person slept 9.5 hours a night. By 1950, that number dropped to 8 hours a night, and today, the average person sleeps under 6.5 hours a night. We are suffering from a lack of sleep on multiple levels.

A poll done by the National Sleep Foundation shows 49% of American adults have sleep-related problems, and one in six has insomnia. Did you know that one of the top prescriptions written by doctors is for sleeping problems?

A study done by the National Institute of Mental Health, in which participants were allowed to sleep as much as they could each night, showed on average that people slept 8.5 hours.

Those who participated in the study felt happier, less fatigued, more creative, energetic, and productive.

God designed us to be stewards of our lives, right? Mind, body, and soul. We need to begin with caring for our bodies, not only with our eating but by getting 7-8 hours of sleep each night – no less. Failure to do so will not only result in fatigue but failure in other areas of our lives, as well.

Tomorrow, I will give some disciplines on sleep.

Day 28

SLEEP
Part 2 of 2

Yesterday, I gave some statistics on sleep. Today, I will get into some disciplines of sleep for the overall importance of optimum health.

Sleep isn't forced. It's an act of surrender and a declaration of trust. By admitting we are not God (who never sleeps), it allows us to accept something that is a truth. We can't make ourselves sleep, but we can create conditions necessary for sleep. Disciplines are wise practices that allow God to teach, train, and heal us. Sleep is a form of discipline.

Try these exercises to develop healthier sleep patterns.

1. For just one day, try to sleep until you cannot sleep anymore. Get out of bed only when you feel you can't possibly sleep any longer. You may need to ask for the help of others to achieve this, but do it. Your body needs this.

2. Go to bed at the same time each night.

3. Don't engage in activities that increase stress. Watching TV and spending time on your computers or cell phone, the elimination of these before bed will do wonders for sleeping.

4. Avoid spicy foods and caffeine in the evenings.

5. Don't force yourself to fall asleep. If you aren't feeling drowsy, read a book, meditate on a Psalm, or turn on soft music. Tossing and turning in bed is not good. Get up and out of bed until you feel drowsy.

6. If you awaken in the middle of the night and don't "have" to get up, stay in bed and give your body a chance to fall back asleep.

Even with tips and discipline, some may have trouble sleeping. It may be helpful to seek a sleep expert for advice, but please don't turn to medication as the solution to your problem with sleeping. Perhaps visiting a counselor or therapist for underlying emotional issues may be a solution for you.

Remember, we cannot make our bodies sleep. We need to create the conditions necessary for sleep.

By regularly practicing some of the tips I've listed, it may get you on a routine of sleeping better to give you the optimal health you need when it comes to rest.

Day 29

ANCHOR YOUR SOUL

There are many things we can do to hold fast when storms hit. I choose to be alone and quiet with God. I rarely care for the opinions of others during these times, but that's just me. I go right to the source for my answers: God's Word.

When you battle despair, disillusionment, and unbelief, you may feel pulled towards the world and what it offers to you. People may try to sway you and things may distract you, but don't let go of what you know to be true. Anchor your soul to the promises of God.

Promises you know to be true. Don't look for shortcuts that veer you away from the storm. Be willing to face the storm with God's best for you. How will you know what that is?

Don't listen to the voice of the enemy when God seems to be silent. Let the anchor of your soul tighten your grip and allow Him to see you through the storm. Remember, when you stand upon the very word of God, He backs His promises with the honor of His name. He is your Anchor. Remember in the darkness what God told you in the light. "Don't doubt in the darkness what God has shown you in the light," is how my friend stated it to me. Don't allow your heart to well up with the fear of doubt. This is where you need to stay tender to the things of God.

The Anchor of your Soul will allow you to deal with issues that surface from time to time. He tells us that. Humble yourself and do the work of sorting through your obstacles. God will give you the strength to endure. Ask Him for it. Say out loud, "Lord, I need strength…your strength."

By anchoring your soul, know that in due time, your breakthrough will come.

"I would have lost heart, unless I had believed that I would see the goodness of the Lord in the land of the living." (*New King James Version*, Psalm 27:13)

Don't lose sight of the fact that God loves you and me. He is with us and has given us authority over our storms. Even though the elements of the storms rise against us, they don't have the power to take us out!

Anchor your soul. Regardless of how you feel or what your circumstances suggest, anchor your soul to the unconquerable force who has your back through every storm you face or may be facing right now. Will your anchor hold? Remember, we may lose sight of God, but He never loses sight of us!

Day 30

SEEK YE FIRST

God tells us that we are to make the principles of God's kingdom our primary priority and concern. I am learning this on my daily walk with Jesus. To live the abundant life we desire, we must first seek His kingdom and His righteousness, and all these things will be given to you, as well. (Matthew 6:33)

Seeking the kingdom first is the cure for all the typical human struggles we face, such as anger, lust, judging others, etc. We continually need to strive to look to God and what He is doing throughout our lives. We shouldn't face our trials and troubles with fear or anxiety, but with trust that God will work in them along with you.

Many things may compete for our attention and take our focus off "seeking first". Be careful. Sometimes we can focus all our attention on something or someone else that becomes a distraction for us, taking our eyes off seeking first the kingdom of God. These could be masked as "somethings" with good intentions, and we become distracted from following through with ultimately seeking God's kingdom. We can be taken far off the "seeking path" by allowing interferences without even realizing it.

When we are concerned with God and His kingdom, we will naturally start to do things that are needed, like volunteering, taking care of our spouse and family, and maintaining a household. While getting involved in the life that God calls us to, we can – and often – allow these "somethings" to take us off course. If we put them ahead of the kingdom, "somethings" can become idols in our lives, even though they are good things.

I learned this lesson in my personal life many years ago. I never realized my husband, my home, or my friends could become idols. Although they are good things, at one point in my life, they took all my attention from God. I eventually lost them all. That's the quick account.

Jesus says with such clarity and authority, "Seek first the kingdom of God." The kingdom is never in trouble. Our lives are only strong and vibrant if lived within the principles of God's kingdom. This is a crucial word of truth for you. Thank God our wins and losses don't define us.

Regarding the troubles I faced at that time in my life with losing my marriage, my home, and many friends, God taught me how to respond to those troubles one by one. Jesus says the kingdom only operates in the present moment. We are to live abundantly in the kingdom today. We can't live in it tomorrow. So, worrying about tomorrow is a useless distraction. I became distracted. I learned that as I count on God today, I can count on Him tomorrow, too, if He permits. My point is, I don't live in the tomorrows anymore and striving for more. I live in today with God. God is teaching me how to respond to both today's happiness and troubles, because God is working with me and alongside me continuously. He has wisely ordered and measured to me what I can handle. I let go of the tomorrows because they may never come. That's up to God.

God continues to show me that I can do all things through Christ who strengthens me, and as I seek first the kingdom of God and His righteousness, all these things will be added unto me…and they are.

Even though I lost a marriage in my past, through seeking God first, many things were restored in my life – a beautiful union with my spouse, a gorgeous home, and more friends than I could have ever imagined. I've been blessed beyond measure from seeking God first.

If you are struggling with what is taking all your attention or focus off of God, I encourage you to stop it!

"But seek ye first the kingdom of God, and his righteousness; and all these things shall be added unto you." (*King James Version*, Matthew 6:33)

I could never imagine my life now without seeking Him first. I encourage you to memorize and follow Matthew 6:33 daily. Don't take your focus off what should always be first in your life every day.

Day 31

SABBATH

When you hear the word Sabbath, you may connect it with being a specific day of the week – maybe a Sunday – and it could involve an act such as going to church. That description could constitute Sabbath for many, and it used to for me.

Not only is honoring the Sabbath important; it's a commandment. What does keeping the Sabbath mean to you?

Keeping the Sabbath is a form of spiritual exercise for many. Sabbath rest is giving up our control and giving it to God, then learning to live on His generosity of the blessings falling all around us. There are many beautiful things to observe when we open our eyes.

Sabbath removes us from playing God in our own lives. It allows God to take care of us while we relax and enjoy the life He has given us. But, how many of us take time to do this?

This is why sleep is so important; we let go totally and trust. We are surrendering our control of thought throughout the time of sleep, and we don't know if it's all going to be well or not.

Keeping the Sabbath is also about being joyful and content.

Another thing to think about is this, Jesus did not keep the Sabbath legalistically. Many times, he performed actions on the Sabbath.

"The sabbath was made for humankind, and not humankind for the sabbath; so, the Son of man is Lord even of the sabbath." (*New Revised Standard Version*, Mark 2:27-28)

Start small with a couple of practices of keeping the Sabbath. Examples of things to do that would be helpful:

Take some time and plan out your Sabbath day. Name your day, because it does not have to be on a Sunday necessarily. What things will you do? What will you eat?

Possibly plan a special meal for you and your family. Invite some friends and start with a special prayer. Make the meal special by involving everyone at the table, telling them how special they are to you.

Play games on your Sabbath. Eat good food that you love. If your day is a Sunday, go to church together.

Try not to make others work, and if possible, make plans for your meal the night before so all the work is done.

Read a book. Write in a journal. Spend time reading the Bible.

Practice hospitality.

Any day can be the Sabbath. Jewish people and Seventh-day Adventists recognize Saturday as their Sabbath. Most Christians observe it on Sunday, the day of the week when the Lord rose from the grave. It's most easy for Christians because that day is typically given off in a workweek and therefore can be a day of rest. My belief is the Sabbath can be any day that is right for you, but please observe one. For most pastors, Sunday is probably the last day on their minds for them to experience rest!

Whatever your day, remember the abundant life calls for honoring the fourth commandment: *"Remember the sabbath day, to keep it Holy."* (*New King James Version*, Exodus 20:8)

Enter your day of rest including your Savior always. Talk to Him, commune with Him, and show love to Him. Honor Him with your life, and encourage others to do the same by your example.

Day 32

ABUNDANT LIFE

Many of us are a prisoner of our past. How do we put our past regrets and shames behind us? Can we ever live a day free of condemnation? Sometimes it seems far from our reach.

We need to believe deep down in the depths of our souls who we are. Do we ever wonder who we are created to be? Believing that our Savior paid our entire debt is the beginning. When we do, we allow freedom and wholesome living to engage us in our faith. When this begins to happen, so much more will start to follow.

Conquering sin can be an uphill climb for us. How often do we do things we lament over only to punish ourselves continuously for doing them?

When we stumble or even fall, it's quite clear the enemy likes to kick us when we're down. It's not easy to combat this.

Consider what Christ went through while enduring the cross for us. He experienced pain yet endured much opposition and ridicule from sinners.

God tells us of an abundant way of life. His love and abundant-life promises are true. How do we receive those abundant life promises?

Pray, ask for forgiveness, and turn away from your attachment to sins that oppress you. Renew your mind and walk freely with your Savior. If we continue to do this daily until we walk freely, we will step right into an abundant way of living. When we know and understand, we can redefine our circumstances and stand against the taunts of the enemy.

When the POWER of the living God is alive within you, you will be able to do exceedingly abundantly more than you could ever ask or imagine. (Ephesians 3:20) Yes, abundant life is yours for the taking. Surrendering is the first step into abundant life.

Day 33

SMILES THROUGH TEARS

Some of us have painful regrets from our past. Mistakes that may leave us feeling hurt, guilty, miserable, shameful, and broken. Your brokenness does not define you.

You are the one in whom Christ dwells, my friend. You are meant to house the fullness of God in every way. God will use you in these life storms if you open your heart to his purpose in you.

Are you struggling to be perfect? Do you live with a deep sense of failure and self-hatred? Remember, you are the one in whom Christ dwells. Your glory is not in what you've done but in who you are.

If you are wounded, please understand that in your weakness is where God's power is revealed in you. We can minister out of our brokenness. We can encourage others through what we've experienced, because through our vulnerability is where Christ shines most brightly. I write this from experience and ask you to consider this.

There is a world out there that's looking for smiles through tears. There is a need for men and women who know the heart of God to reach out and show a spirit of forgiveness, caring, and possibly offer help in healing to another.

The New Testament approaches Christian life by telling us who we are and whose we are. It encourages us to live in a manner worthy of that identity.

Don't remain stagnant in your struggles. Think about being a vessel used by God today. Smile through those tears and allow God to use your pain with a purpose, embracing someone who needs your experience to encourage them. By helping others in their lives and turning your brokenness into glorifying God, He will give you smiles through tears, and your ability to be used will bring everlasting joy in your healing process.

Day 34

STRONGHOLDS

Often our days can start with wrong thoughts. Lies we've been told that hurt us, thoughts we think may harm us or eventually even destroy us.

A stronghold is an incorrect thinking pattern that has molded itself into our way of thinking. They can affect our feelings and how we respond to situations in our lives. Strongholds can be powerfully misleading, as they are built on deception and error. Often our past mistakes and even current choices allow these strongholds to continue.

What goes into our minds comes out in our lives. If you can't control what you think, it's difficult to control what you do.

God's Word tells us to take every thought captive. Your life will always move in the direction of your strongest thoughts. 2 Corinthians 10:4 tells us to cast down imaginations and very high things that exalt itself against the knowledge of God and bring into captivity every thought to the obedience of Christ.

As you face the day, engage your brain in only positive thoughts. It's easy for our minds to think positive thoughts.

As we meditate and wash our minds with God's Word, we can become transformed by renewing our minds. We can combat these wrong thought patterns by fighting them with God, shielding us against those wrong thoughts. It's a battle. Meditating and washing will allow you to know the will of God and discern what is right, perfect, and good in your life.

Deception from the stronghold will not stand a chance if the areas of your mind are programmed with the truth from God's Word. That becomes your defense.

Take on the mind of Jesus to diminish any strongholds you may have. Know the truth today, which is God's Word.

"And you will know the truth, and the truth will set you free." (English Standard Version, John 8:32)

Day 35

STINKIN' THINKIN'

Think today about how your attitude and thoughts play a pivotal role in the way you live your life and how they are one of the most significant keys to any successful endeavor.

Unfortunately, I have witnessed the power of a phrase you may have heard about called "stinkin' thinkin'." I've had to monitor this with the loved ones in my life for many years. The phrase may be something you or someone dear to you battles with internally.

People who have a negative attitude have cloudy thinking. It is more common than not for negative words to seep out of us. We may tell ourselves something like, "I've always been fat, so I'll always be fat." This is not a true statement. Instead, change your way of thinking with a more positive statement, such as, "I will make healthier dietary choices and exercise regularly, and the weight will drop off."

Remember, we are body, mind, and spirit. We need to speak out truths and believe them. Sometimes we may need to encourage others around us to speak out their truths, as well. Often, negative thoughts of others can infiltrate our emotions, especially when regularly in the presence of someone with a negative attitude.

"I can do all things through Christ who strengthens me." (*New King James Version*, Philippians 4:13) *"...with God all things are possible."* (*New King James Version*, Matthew 19:26)

We must remove the word can't from our vocabulary and subconscious thinking and reprogram ourselves with an "I will not be denied" attitude. A "can do" type of thinking will take you where you want to go.

If a lie (negative word) enters your mind, grab it, throw it down, stomp on it, and speak the truth in its place. Do this instantly. Instead of referring to yourself as fat and ugly, say to yourself, "I accept myself; I forgive myself, and I love myself."

Always confess the positive and refrain from the negative. Always. Come up with positive affirmations. Write them down; confess them. Say them out loud each morning and every night. Most importantly, be specific with your affirmations. Reprogram yourself with the "can do" thinking, believing you can do this, and you will.

We all need to be grateful for what we have, even if we are without what we believe we want. Accept yourself. Forgive yourself and love yourself each day. Encourage those around you to do the same.

Calling out "stinkin' thinkin'" when you recognize the negativity takes time. You are changing an unhealthy pattern. As you keep pressing forward with this new reprogramming of yourself, you will eventually overcome "stinkin' thinkin'" and be on your way to a more positive way of living and possibly help those around you do the same.

Day 36

DOUBTS IN THE DARKNESS

Whenever we venture out to conquer new ground or fulfill something God has called us to do, why does opposition seem to come?

For me, the enemy stirs up fears and past failures that haunt my mind. God is bringing me through situations, but more times than I care to mention, I doubt in the darkness. Why do I do this? It's because the enemy wants to take my eyes off Christ. Do you ever feel the enemy attacks just before God does something great in your life? That's me in regards to my writing. I started years ago with my writing, and I've been dealing with some of the worst pain I've ever experienced in my life – the pain of heartache. Unfortunately, during these dark times of hurt, I've doubted what my purpose is, and then the doubting of myself started to affect my writing. My thoughts would rise, but then the enemy would attack my mind.

I've felt like I've failed so many people in my lifetime. More and more doubts enter my mind as I struggle with this continuous pain until sometimes, I feel I can't continue. I must combat this with truth because the "Voice of Truth" tells me a different story. When I hear this voice, it's only then that I can hit pause, regroup, and press on.

Whenever the enemy throws these lies my way, it's usually short lived since I can pretty much know the opposite of those lies is true.

If you're like me, you need to silence your fears. Your doubts are your insecurities. Past mistakes, which the enemy uses to taunt us, need to be put to rest.

Being vulnerable for a moment, I will share thoughts of the taunting in my head that sometimes appear:

You were a bad mother. Your children will never love you or respect you. The Voice of Truth tells me a different story, though. (Be kind one to another, tenderhearted, FORGIVING one another as God in Christ forgave you.)

You will never amount to anything. Again, the Voice of Truth tells me a different story. (I can do all things through Christ who strengthens me!)

Many more negative thoughts pop up, and this happens over and over as I doubt in the darkness of my pain.

Scripture describes the enemy as a liar, an accuser, and the source of confusion. Doubts arise because of these attacks.

Understand God has called us to newness in Christ. There is no condemnation in us who are in Christ Jesus. Pray that you will be healed, restored, strengthened, and mobilized. That is what I continuously do through it all. Pray for your walk of faith. Pray for it every day, every hour, and every minute because you need it. Continue this through the "doubts in the darkness" because God will show you the truth in the light. Look to Him. He is your forever source of truth.

As for me, I have life in the Spirit. I walk in the Spirit continuously. My prayer is that for you, also. Jesus will make a public spectacle of powers that oppose us. He went to the place of utter public humiliation for you and me. He won our victory there!

God tells us to forget the past and look forward to what lies ahead. I press on to receive the heavenly prize for which God, through Christ Jesus, is calling us.

God told me to write this book. Any doubts that arise – and trust me, they do – should be stomped out. I'm not allowing the enemy to throw dirt at me. I stop it right away. I make a conscientious effort to seek God at the moment the doubt hits. I do not view myself covered with smudges of past sins. They are gone, wiped clean.

I'm encouraging you today to lay hold of your life, free of condemnation. Free of fear from past failures. What is God calling you to do? Don't doubt in the darkness what God is showing you in the light!

$\mathcal{D}ay$ 37

LOVE YOUR ENEMIES

Can you think of individuals you don't feel like loving but whom you could try to will good words? They may not necessarily be an enemy, but you don't like them for whatever reason. I have some that quickly come to mind, but I don't dwell on that thought. I can't. God says, *"You shall not take vengeance, nor bear any grudge against the children of your people, but you shall love your neighbor as yourself: I am the* LORD.*" (New King James Version,* Leviticus 19:18)

Loving your neighbor was the basic expectation – the minimum standard, but Jesus asks for much more. He commands his people to love their enemies. What does it mean to love someone?

To most people, love is a feeling and emotion. However, the Greek word agapao (or agape) refers not to a feeling but an action. To love (agapao) is to will the good of another. It does not entail an emotion, loving, or even liking a person. Loving our enemies seems impossible for us because we think we can never feel love for a person who abuses or has abused us.

Let's remember that Jesus is not asking us to feel love but to act in love towards everyone, including our enemies.

For me, it's easy to love those who love me, but it's hard to love those who don't like me. It's easy to pray for people I love but not for those who cause me problems. Nonetheless, I do it anyway because this is the way to abundant living in Jesus, by following His lead. I'm sympathizing by saying it can be difficult, I've done it; therefore, I can speak from experience. When we do this, we are behaving as our Father in heaven. (Matthew 5:44)

God loves His enemies by acting for their good. Again, this is an action word. We need to be aware of those who are difficult to love and set our concentration on showing them love.

How can you do this? You can start by praying over them. You might choose to show them an act of kindness that involves doing something for them that would make them happy. Keep in mind that this isn't about you. It's about what Jesus calls us to do. Set aside a little time today and give some of your focus to a person who may be considered difficult for you to love.

Remember, God proves his love for us in that while we were still sinners, Christ died for us. What a victory you could have on your way to abundant living if you can jump this hurdle. For some like me, this may be an Olympic-sized hurdle in your life. You're an overcomer. You can do ALL THINGS through Christ who gives you strength.

Having to step out and do what you think is impossible will prove rewarding when you achieve victory. Reaching for something so difficult can only be done with God's help. We need to pray through every word and every action taken to show love to your enemy. The evil one doesn't want it. He wants to keep you stuck in a frenzy of gossip, hatred, and discord, causing anxiety and suffering in your life.

Jesus, on the other hand, wants us to love our enemies and pray for those who persecute us. (Matthew 5: 43-48) When we love our enemies, we are acting like our Father and Jesus. We are setting ourselves up for abundant living. If Jesus is for you, who can be against you? Use the help He offers you to show love to your enemy. Don't try to do this on your own. When you stand with Him in love and pray for those who have wronged you or offended you, you will see them through the eyes of your Savior, who reconciled you to God through His death.

By Christ dwelling inside you, it gives you strength to follow His example. By not repaying evil for evil but instead extending self-giving, non-resistant love, you are acting like a true disciple, and abundant living is something you will enjoy. Align yourself with God and show the love to that person who He directs you to today. I'm encouraging you as your coach. I've been through this exercise of faith. Your life becomes less of a burden to live out when you can truly love your enemies.

Day 38

RESOLUTIONS

Resolutions are made, and excitement flies high with new goals and new beginnings. We anticipate all the greatness that will come from our decisions. But, days into our resolution, life sometimes gets in our way. It's sad to say there are those who feel discouraged only moments after they mentally resolve into their action. The thought before the action may have been the tallest giant they never expected to face.

Bathing your resolutions in prayer can bring successful turnouts in the long run.

In making our resolutions without any prayer involved, you are telling God you are strong enough to do this without any help from Him. Are any of us so strong that we don't need to rely on God?

Whichever the case, please don't give up!

For those who prayed over their resolutions, you might be wondering if God heard you. Did you commit change to yourself, or did you include God, asking for assistance from him? I'm here to encourage you to include God always in any RESOLUTION you make.

If you have already started a resolution, evaluate how it's going. Did you include God, or did you just put your mind to starting it? Whatever it is, start over, but this time with God. It's never too late, and chances are if you look to Him through the struggles of change, He is right by your side, lending you a Word, a person, or a way to get through to accomplishing your resolve.

Isaiah 55 promises us, like the rain and snow does what it needs to do, it accomplishes God's desires and achieves the purpose for which He sends it.

That means there is POWER in praying God's Word over our resolutions, especially when we feel the battle of change. It's difficult to break a bad habit or form a new routine. We can't see it in the quiet time of our prayer, but the words we raise to heaven are WEAPONS OF WARFARE. Because of our prayers, angels fight with demons to bring about God's will.

God's Word is "living" and active. Sharper than any double-edged sword, it penetrates and even divides soul and spirit, joints and marrow; it judges the thoughts and attitudes of the heart. (Hebrews 4:12)

The Word of God is a part of every Christian's armor. It's saying that we must carry the sword of the Spirit, again stating it is the Word of God. (Ephesians 6:17)

We must know God's word pierces everything it touches; it is never ineffective. That's why it's so important not to make RESOLUTIONS alone. We need to pray and read our bibles daily or listen to The Bible app. I can't go a day without it. God gives us everything we need to tap into His POWER and stand in our RESOLUTIONS with strength. When you do, God promises great things will happen.

When we don't include God, my friends, it's like watching a war zone in a movie. My husband and I watched *Zookeeper's Wife*. The family and their animals were shot at from every direction. A true warzone in front of our face as we watched it all play out.

When we pray and include God in our changes, He is alongside us in the war zone, appropriating His Power on our behalf. The struggle is difficult, friends. Don't doubt that, but please don't give up quickly if you feel challenged. Remember your goals and declare the Word of God within your prayers. By doing so, you will have a powerful weapon that no enemy or addiction can penetrate. I encourage you to press forward in making your RESOLUTIONS. Our great Leader will lead you all the way.

The only reason I am still able to carry on my healthy lifestyle to this day is because of prayer. It's a daily struggle. At times, it's easier than others, but always with God's help, I am certain that challenges can be overcome. Praise God!

My hope and prayer are that you may have something brought to your mind that needs a resolution! Act on it, but do it with God alongside you.

Day 39

OVERCOMMITTING

Hurrying and distractions are nothing new. In fact, in our age, we seem to have perfected them. We become obsessed with productivity, efficiency, and speed. Many things we do must be done fast, but why? Because we overcommit ourselves. We drive fast, eat fast, and even love fast so we can fit into our schedules all that life throws at us.

While certain cultures believe haste makes waste, we are a culture surrounded by things that remind us that speed reflects power and success. The more we can take on and perfect within a short amount of time, the higher the position we can attain in our status. While this may be true, it seems to me as we increasingly move faster, the less we are enjoying life.

Possibly, this could be because we overcommit.

One way to counteract this is to be present where we are.

Jesus did not say much about being in a hurry, busyness, or even distractions. He did allow us to learn from the story of the two sisters, Mary and Martha, who lived with their brother Lazarus. Jesus stayed with them when he was in town.

Jesus had his disciples come for dinner, and Martha began to panic. She had too much to do and not enough time to do it. Her sister chose not to help with preparations but instead sat at the feet of Jesus and listened to his teaching. Martha confronted Mary about this and asked Jesus to scold her for not helping. (Luke 10:40)

Being overcommitted, too busy, or preoccupied are not new to our society today. Will we take on too many things and be concerned about the wrong things, missing out on the important stuff?

We have quickened our pace of life only to become less patient. We may not be spontaneous anymore because of overcommitting, and therefore, we rob ourselves of joy that could come in the present moment.

How did we allow ourselves to get into this predicament? Only we can answer that if this speaks to us.

You should not rush some things. One way we can spell the word love is T-I-M-E. If we realize overcommitting is an issue, we can stop saying yes to everything that comes our way.

Learn to enjoy the present moment. Where God has you right now is your present moment. Be aware of your attitude and the kindness you show to others. In our spiritual lives, we can't do anything important in a hurry or overcommit ourselves. We rob God, ourselves, and those around us of T-I-M-E. We need to eliminate the bad things from our lives in order to slow down and find balance.

Throughout today, I highly encourage you to see if there are things that can be eliminated from your schedule to allow more time for the most important things – those that can last eternally. Remember, you should prepare like Martha so you can worship like Mary.

BE STILL

"Be still before the Lord, all mankind..." (*New International Version,* Zechariah 2:13)

Wait quietly in God's presence while His thoughts form silently in the depths of your soul.

I spoke this out loud to God this morning, as I know His presence is here with me even as I write for you today.

With all the busyness yet fun surrounding my days of late, I know my time with God could become compromised a little. I'm sure many of us experience what I may be feeling when life is flying by so quickly. Just recently, I took time to enjoy a vacation and deepen some relationships that have added such value to my life. However, during the time, I felt my total quiet time and alone time with God had been somewhat missed.

It's not bad that our lives are so busy these days unless we are absent from the presence of God. We need to recharge deeper on some days when we know our spiritual health is in need.

God is the Creator of the Universe, yet He chooses to make His humble home in our hearts. When we are rushing around, the hurrying keeps our hearts earthbound, don't you agree? God wants to know us intimately, and it's in the stillness that He can speak to us with "Holy whispers". If we can't ever stay still, how can we quiet our minds to hear the still, small voice inside of us?

This morning, I asked God to quiet my mind, settle me down to focus once again, and allow me to hear Words of Life...peace and love that I know He wants me to experience and that I so desperately need. I want to use this for furthering His ministry, but how can I if I don't recharge?

We can turn our spiritual health on by tuning our hearts at some point each day to receive messages of God's abundant blessings for us. We must search for them in the still, quiet moments as He says in his Word. Lay your requests before God and wait in expectation. (Psalm 5:3) I feel I've been able to accomplish this.

This is written to you and prayed over. That's what I choose to do. I must work on tasks every day. They are stored in my mind, knowing I need to accomplish them. It's always a relief when I can finish them with God's help.

"Be still and know that I am God." (*New International Version*, Psalm 46:10)

There is no emotion we can experience that's better than being in the still presence of God. There is an emotion of peace in the stillness. That is pure comfort. Let this simmer in your thoughts as you head into your day.

Day 41

LIVING WITHOUT ANGER

There are different types of anger. Some are acceptable, such as the "righteous anger" that God describes in His Word, and other anger not so much. Living an abundant life within God's kingdom allows us to manage the uncontrollable anger.

You can work on uncontrolled anger that affects many wonderful human beings. This undesirable emotion is a common type of anger – one that can strike us immediately. When someone accidentally spills hot coffee on you, you might react out of anger. It happens quickly, and our bodies respond. You aren't happy, and your emotions flare up.

Another anger which is damaging to our soul is the kind that grows over some time. The more we stew on a situation, the worse it becomes because your thoughts get involved.

These are two fits of anger, and two ingredients fuel them: unmet expectations and fear. Both can unite into a powerful emotion. I've examined these two culprits for years in my own life.

Unmet expectations can cause anger. Say someone is late for your lunch date. You might experience mild irritation or worry, but by adding fear into the equation, it ignites. *Why is my friend late? They don't care about me,* is what you might think.

By being late without a good reason, it shows a lack of respect. So, your anger starts to stir. Then fear arises. We fear we're not important to that person, and the unmet expectation moves to a level of threat.

Life is full of unmet expectations, and we can't control them. What we can control is managing our fears. We can do this by walking with God. We need to examine where our anger comes from and replace the "lie or fear" about it with the truth.

Often fear is the need to be in control.

- I am alone.
- Things must always go as I want them to.
- Something terrible will happen if I make a mistake.
- I must be perfect all the time
- I need to anticipate everything that will happen to me.

These are all examples telling us that we must be in control all the time. The fear is if we are not in control, things will go badly and our anger becomes loud. Again, this is something I've learned over many years.

Let's replace fear with the POWER OF GOD!

- You are never alone.
- Jesus is in control.
- Mistakes happen all the time, but things usually work out fine.
- Jesus accepts me even though I am not perfect.

Truth is based on the reality of the presence and POWER of God. Living an abundant life is available to all. Living inside the kingdom of God allows Him to protect us and fight for our well-being. When this happens, our anger diminishes.

We can go from fear to trust. When we live close to God, He informs us. We can trust our heavenly Father.

Remember today, be slow to anger. (James 1:19) Give yourself grace. Change is gradual. As long as we continue to work on exchanging lies for truth, we engage in spiritual exercises. As a result, we will see changes in our behavior. Anger will diminish, and understanding will take its place. Breathe a sigh of relief and know you are not alone in dealing with this emotion. Give it over to your Savior, He loves you, and perfect love casts out all fear.

Day 42

TURN THE OTHER CHEEK?

How many of us will be cursed or persecuted this week, beaten up, laughed at, or even sued? Hopefully none of us, but when and if it comes to these occasions, how are we to respond? Turn the other cheek?

If you're wronged in any way, what does God say to do instead of retaliating? Jesus asks us to bless those who harm us. Can you think of any enemies you may have that are rising against you or actively pursuing your demise?

Jesus answers, *"But I tell you, do not resist an evil person. If anyone slaps you on the right cheek, turn them the other cheek also. And if anyone wants to sue you and take your shirt, hand over your coat as well."* (*New International Version*, Matthew 5:39-40)

Turning the other cheek does not imply pacifism nor does it mean we place ourselves in mortal danger. Turning the other cheek means not returning insult for insult in retaliation, which is what most people expect and how people of the world often act.

Responding to hatred with love is what we are instructed to do. When we react in a manner that is unnatural, we can then glorify

God because it displays the supernatural indwelling power of the Holy Spirit within us.

Think about praying for the success of your competitor. (Anyone whose success in some way diminishes yours). Ask God to reveal these people to you. It doesn't usually take long to figure this out. Once you do, pray over them. It's funny, but once you begin praying for them, you may realize an inner tension occurring because we don't want them to succeed. The more you press through and pray from your heart over them, something strange begins to happen. Mark these words, when you do feel the supernatural in you occurring, you'll appreciate the wisdom of Jesus and His commands to pray for your enemies and turn the other cheek.

Try turning this activity into training. Spend a few minutes a day praying for your competitors whoever they may be. Think of them this moment. Hold that person up before God and pray multiple good things over this person or these people in your life. Be specific. Watch and see through the days and weeks ahead how your heart will begin to change for that person or the people. I've done this exercise myself, and the power through prayer works.

By praying over others, you will soon find yourself looking at your competition with love instead of turning the other cheek.

Day 43

JUST SAY NO

I see myself living in this contemporary type of society these days, and I understand certain kinds of societies have been around for centuries in different ways. But why does it seem so prevalent in today's society that we're seeing so many things flashing in front of our eyes that others feel we should be informed about? I'm speaking of a society that seems to be obsessed with sexuality, lust, and many other forms of what I refer to as scary distractions. Our magazines are dripping with it. Our television programs are obsessed with it, and much of our music is nothing short of lust covered with so-called love. We are fascinated with sexuality.

On the other hand, Christians as well as Jews – and even non-religious yet morally concerned people – have tried to stand against culture and maintain the position that purity, integrity, and fidelity are essential.

We can go to church to pray, sing hymns, and set our minds on things in heaven like a Christian is taught, but then we come home and watch the news, check social media, and expose ourselves to television shows, commercials, and movies full of sex, violence, and devastation. I don't know about you, but this can easily drag me down. So, how can we overcome?

Living in a life of abundance with God, we learn God is good, and we learn to see everything through God's eyes. Too many people try and fail to deal with struggles faced by what they see at a glance in contemporary living – lust, perversions of truth, and more. Through their willpower and tearful prayers, they try but find no genuine change of what they've succumbed to. We can't change our hearts by merely changing our outer behavior alone. Does "just saying no" work?

Jesus says if our eye offends us, pluck it out. Unfortunately, we wouldn't have any body parts if everything that offended us had to be cut off.

Walking with God, we know who we are and whose we are. You will never be free from what has its hooks in you until you find something you want more. It's about giving ourselves over to bigger, better, and more powerful desires. Again, as I've shared, I've been through this, I've experienced it.

Now to Him who is able to do exceedingly, abundantly above all we ask or think, according to the power that works in us. (*New King James Version,* Ephesians 3:20)

Life isn't about quieting down or repressing your God-given life force. It's about filtering, focusing, and turning it on something beautiful.

Just saying no to the sins that so easily trip us up is a start, but when we resolve ourselves to be an apprentice of Jesus, we begin to change our behavior. Countless people have overcome struggles, but when you have a desire to change, a desire to emulate Jesus, and He becomes your source of satisfaction through prayer, you are on your first steps of real and lasting change.

Today, remember to say no to the lures that will set you up for failure. However, say yes to the intimacy, love, and POWER of what Jesus can do through you.

Day 44

LIVE WITHOUT LYING

Have you ever said "I swear" or "I promise" when trying to get others to believe you? What about comments like "I swear to God I didn't mean it" or "I promise I'll take the trash out later"? Why did you use those certain words to get your point across?

What keeps us from lying? The question is probing. I think lying is wrong, and like most people, I don't want anyone to lie to me. It offers minimal gain at high risks. There must be something that drives this behavior in me and others. I don't want to lie, and I'm sure you don't either. Still, we all lie a lot and more than we realize because we often rationalize and justify our deceptions, right? I had to think about this myself.

- No, you don't look fat in those jeans.
- Yes, let's get together soon
- I'll be praying for you.
- No, he's not available right now.

There are shocking studies which conclude we are lied to on an average of two hundred times in a day. Studies say Americans lie to their children regularly. If research on this subject is credible, nearly all of us tell lies and more often than we realize.

Many of us don't want to deal with someone else's hurt feelings. We mean no harm in just telling a "white lie". They don't want to get in trouble, so lying becomes justifiable.

I feel we will lie to get what we want or avoid something we don't want. If life is "all about us", then lying is justifiable. Life is not just about us, though, no matter what you have been programmed to believe. When we believe that lie, we are unfortunately destroying the integrity of our souls by thinking we were created to please only ourselves.

Jesus says in Mark 8:36, Even if we gain the whole world and lose our soul, we have truly lost what is most important. God tells us not to swear falsely but carry out our vows made to the Lord. He also says, do not swear at all: either by heaven, for it is the throne of God, or by earth, for it is His footstool. Let your words be 'Yes' or 'No'. (Matthew 5:33-37)

Jesus talks about the issue of swearing, meaning making a verbal promise or an oath.

Jesus is always aiming for something higher for us. He wants us always to speak the truth. A new kind of person with a new type of character. If we are walking hand in hand daily with Jesus, we begin putting away falsehood; we speak the truth always.

Become the person who naturally tells the truth. If you do this often and consistently, people will not need you to swear by anything because you always speak the truth. God has given you the ability to speak. Learn how to let your yes be yes and be able to bless and be blessed. Live without lying in any form. Speak the truth in love, and remember what Paul says to the Colossians,

"Do not lie to each other, since you have taken off your old self with its practices." (*New International Version*, Colossians 3:9)

Take this with you today and make a conscientious effort to be a light to others. Live without lying, allow others to trust you more, and *"Let your light shine before men, that they may see your good works and glorify your Father in heaven."* (*New King James Version*, Matthew 5:16)

$\mathcal{D}ay\,45$

VANITY

The world measures our worth based on our appearance, production, and performance, which seem to be the only things that count as we walk through life in this shallow shell of a world.

We all want to be loved. We groan for it. We are born to seek praise and recognition. So how does vanity get a hold of us and can we combat it?

Regardless of our physical appearance, talents, and abilities, we are each an amazing creation in the image of God. The world doesn't tell us this, though. They show off that we praise success, idolize beauty, and applaud those who have it. Are we one of those?

Recognition of something you've accomplished allows you to feel good about yourself, right? Unfortunately, this moment is only temporary. We are only as good as our next performance, and it becomes a vicious cycle of repetitive actions.

Think about this, how often do people try to take themselves to a higher level once they've achieved recognition from something they've set out to do? Vanity is rooted in our insecurities and driven by our need for affirmation by others. How many times do we accomplish something and immediately want others to know about it? We keep others from knowing our weaknesses and failures, but we broadcast our success. In conversations, we try to be humble. However, we really have an agenda, wishing the other person would know how great we are, and then subtly, we find ways to interject our success into our humble conversations. Trust me, I've done this in my past. You are not walking alone if you can relate.

Beware of vanity! You will receive no rewards from your heavenly Father for this.

"So when you give to the poor, do not sound a trumpet before you, as the hypocrites do in the synagogue and in the streets, so that they may be honored by men. Truly I say to you, they have their reward in full. But when you give to the poor, do not let your left hand know what your right hand is doing, so that you're giving will be in secret. Then your Father, who sees what is done in secret, will reward you." (*New American Standard Bible,* Matthew 6:2-4)

Don't be tempted to let others know about your good works. We need to practice this. Don't allow vanity to have a place in your life. Recognize it, fight it, and remember, your heavenly Father who sees in secret will reward you. There is no need to seek the applaud and approval of others by allowing vanity to creep into the doors of your heart. Dismiss it with the humble knowledge that your reward will come from God.

Be aware that in the book of Ecclesiastes, the word vanity appears in twenty-nine verses and five of those times are in Ecclesiastes 1:2. Vanity of vanities, says the preacher. Vanity of vanities! All is vanity. Why does this appear so many times? We need to take heed that this is a warning, that's why. Be aware of how you receive recognition.

Again, my friend, let's not allow vanity any place in our lives. God is clear on this. Enjoy your blessings from your heavenly Father and give all glory to His name. After all, He deserves the credit because He's the one who created you.

Day 46

JUDGING

Many of us have been judged unfairly and criticized in our lives. It feels awful and produces nothing short of anger and hurt. When we judge others, we criticize them. Correcting someone can be a healthy action, even life-enhancing. However, judging others never is. We need to understand the difference.

Many times, we judge others to make us feel better about ourselves, or there are times we try to "fix" people. Often, these two are done together. We may act as though our intentions are good, but when we judge others, we care more about ourselves than that other person. When I witness judgment inflicted on a person, and it works in the way of making them recoil, get angry, or even cry, I see a strong weapon rising in one's arsenal. I'm sad to say I've witnessed this time and again within my own family. The one doing the judging only gets more powerful through feeling they've victimized yet another and made themselves look "high and mighty" in the process. Though judging works in some cases, it fails more often than not.

Judging does not flow from a heart of love. When we judge, we force others to recognize their errors. As in the case of my family, this type of judgment is generally not received well. It may come in the form of "joking around" or it can come as "care and concern", but to those judged, they feel attacked and rightfully so. They often fight back, become defensive, or as with myself, I tend to bury it all deep within and feel the intense hurt by inflicted pain. This is not healthy.

Judging can tear a person down, and often there is no one around to build them back up. The old saying "don't judge a person until you've walked a mile in their shoes" is the truth. None of us know their past struggles, what they are facing, or even what may have led them to the "act" they are being judged on or disagreed with over.

Many times, judging a person makes one feel better about themselves. It's the reason gossip may feel good to some. Judging others puts us on the "moral high ground" and diminishes others.

Jesus tells us, *"Do not judge, and you will not be judged."* (*New International Version*, Luke 6:37)

The measure you give will be the measure you get. Jesus makes a point that if you judge someone, be prepared to be judged in return. We are displaying hypocrisy when we judge others. The Bible speaks about getting the log out of your eye before trying to get the speck out of someone else's. Yikes! Who are we to judge? Jesus gives ample reasons not to judge. It provokes anger, it prevents us from being able to help others, and both are something that takes us off the path of truly loving one another.

Pray for those who you feel need judgment. Seek Jesus and communicate to the person that they are not alone.

"So in everything, do to others what you would have them do to you, for this sums up the law and the Prophets." (*New International Version*, Matthew 7:12), which is known as The Golden Rule.

I hope this encouragement allows each of us to pause and think our words through instead of being quick to speak on someone else's faults or failures.

Day 47

POVERTY MINDSET

Jesus told the rich, young ruler that to inherit eternal life, he should give all his money to the poor and follow Jesus. (Luke 18:18-23) I have heard many people in my lifetime talk about this passage. Does this mean we should be willing to give up everything we have and take on a poverty mindset?

I don't believe God wants us to live in poverty or as beggars. I think God wants us to live with adequate materials and necessary provision for ourselves and our families. This includes a place to live, food, clothing, insurance, and even having enough money for recreation and vacation. There is nowhere I read in scripture that there is a conflict between abundant living in God's kingdom and using our money to have a comfortable life. Poverty is not spiritual; it's the lack of a certain amount of material possessions or money, says Wikipedia.

What does adequate necessary provision look like to you? Did you know over 90% of the world's population can't afford a car? In our western culture, cars are not luxuries; they are considered a part of adequate necessary provision. Most people live without homes, medical insurance, and retirement accounts, while many of us feel they are adequate necessary provisions. If we are trying to acquire these necessities, it makes the question "how much we should give away" a little more difficult to answer. Although many of us have more than we need, most people lack what they need.

The longer we live in the kingdom of God, the more we will discover the needs of the world. Living in a country of abundance during an age of excessive living, we have become so desensitized to others' needs. The more we live in the light of God's words, the more able we are to give out of our abundance with a cheerful heart.

I've had the privilege of traveling to other countries to see what poverty looks like, but living in a country where excess is abundant, poverty mindsets still surface around me regularly.

Involving the proper perspective about wealth and knowing it's a provision from God, we must not treat it as a god. We should ask ourselves questions like, *Do I need this?*

Will it bring joy to serving God? Remember, Paul counsels us that there is great gain in godliness combined with contentment. (1 Timothy 6:6)

We aren't called to give everything away either and hold on to a poverty mindset. Living in God's kingdom requires wisdom, and we are not supposed to hold a poverty mindset. However, we are to understand Jesus's teachings of example, such as to love God, self, and neighbor.

Examine ways we spend money, how we think of possessions and see them through God's eyes. Ask yourself questions when you are hesitant about making a purchase.

Do you need that new watch that just went on sale but is still too expensive, especially for daily use? While looking through the lens of life with God by your side, you may answer a lot of questions before making your purchase. Am I spending too much on this and not allowing adequate money for my ministry?

I'm finding that if I look at it as being all God's money, I'm less likely to spend God's money on something I don't need. However, I won't say I never do it. I'm a child of God who lives an abundant life and is not under law. I don't hold a poverty mindset because I am a Christ follower. I use the wisdom that God continues to give me because I ask Him for it daily. He directs me on what to give away as well as where there is a need. If you ask this for your own lives, God will lead you, also.

A poverty mindset is not fitting of a Christ follower. We are to live an abundant life in order to help those around us who need help. God will speak to you on what to give away. Ask Him.

JUDGING YOURSELF

How often do we do this to ourselves? It is not healthy to judge or even evaluate ourselves. It's not our role. Please don't compare yourself with other people either. It's understandable how difficult this has become in a Facebook/Instagram world. By comparing, we are producing pride or even inferiority.

Each of us is different in how it affects us. Comparing is not only wrong, but it's also meaningless. I often find myself comparing as I scroll through Facebook posts, only to catch what I'm doing and then correct my thinking.

We can't look for affirmations in the wrong places, like from our evaluations or those of other people. The only source of real affirmation is the unconditional love God has for us.

Sometimes we view God as an angry judge looking for our faults and failures. I found this more to be true as I was growing up, but now as I walk through life, I see nothing can be further from the truth. God is love. If He disciplines us (and we know when that is), it's never in anger or disgust. It's only to prepare us for seeing Him face to face and living in an eternal state with Him.

"For God did not send his Son into the world to condemn the world, but to save the world through Him." (*New International Version,* John 3:17)

We ought not to condemn ourselves. We should not judge ourselves either.

Do not judge, and you will not be judged. Do not condemn, and you will not be condemned. Forgive and you will be forgiven. This verse is found in Luke 6:37.

We need to live out Luke 6:37 every day despite how difficult this can be. We are overcomers!

For your health, try to love yourself more and forgive your shortcomings. Then pass the freedom and happiness it brings on to others in need. Try speaking this truth into someone you love today. It could bring the freedom they may have been searching for.

Day 49

WORRY

I often speak to myself while writing these daily coaching files. I think about the times I worry about things and how things typically work themselves out for the good. I just experienced this again while getting ready for an event in our home.

I must breathe a sigh of relief when all ends up working out and it's over. But, what it does to me while going through the planning is not a good thing. I am speaking to myself here but hopefully for your benefit.

None of us can add a single moment to our lives by worrying. It's the opposite. We lose life when we worry. I know this and believe I understand this, but often, I don't remedy it. I spend the time worrying, and it causes health issues that could eventually shorten my life.

We are told by God not to worry. We can find freedom from anxieties just by spending time with God. I know how it often calms my soul when I take a quiet moment to sit and reflect with God, basking in His presence.

"When anxiety was great within me, your consolation brought me joy." (*New International Version*, Psalm 94:19)

I admonish myself when I acknowledge that if I'm anxious, I am not trusting God. I am not. I turn it around and remember how God proves his faithfulness to me. He will never leave me alone; He is always with me. Thankfully, this is pure truth. There is a passage I read (Luke 12:29-31) that may help you as it did me.

God tells us that we don't need to be anxious about anything; just pray about EVERYTHING. (Philippians 4:6)

Don't allow your brain to tell you it's too small for God. Prayer is that powerful connection with the One who is the source of our comfort, strength, and hope.

There is a saying I've heard before that I'll share with you and encourage you to do. For your health, my friends, "Take your worries about the future to the One who holds the future in His hands."

He's got the whole world in His hands, and that most definitely means you're included!

Day 50

HOLDING PATTERN

You may have heard the term "holding pattern" in aviation. It's a holding maneuver designed to delay an aircraft that's already in flight while keeping it within a specified air space. Let's think about this when it comes to waiting on God in our lives. We are the planes waiting in airspace; He is the Air Traffic Controller who sees what we do not.

Sometimes we may feel we are in this type of "holding pattern" in our lives as if everything has just stopped. We then feel the need to surrender our dreams because we think God didn't acknowledge them. That's not necessarily the case. God could be saying, "Wait on me."

When God seems silent over something in your life, sense His nearness to you. He's your silent partner. He's your Air Traffic Controller. He sees what you do not see.

Allow God to speak to you through this holding pattern in your life. It could be a defining time for you. Though defining times are difficult, God uses them for our protection.

We may go into the "holding pattern" kicking and screaming, "You gave me a dream, Lord! I trusted you! Nothing's happening, and I feel like a fool!" If you trust Him, you'll come out of this season leaning on the Everlasting Arms.

The Lord may be asking you to wait because He's making you ready. I can relate to this, having lived in solitude for years between marriages. When I prayed for a husband, it took years. I felt alone, isolated, and unheard. I prayed but no answers. Little did I know, God had to remove the very things from me that the enemy could have used against me. It took time to discover what those things in my life were. I learned I had to embrace the loneliness, find contentment, and understand that God was my safest place. He was my refuge. He was my "go to" in times of trouble. He was the lover of my soul.

"Be still and know that He is God" (*New International Version,* Psalm 46:10)

God knows what is in us and what can hurt us later. He'll never send us out unprepared; He's very protective over us. God began to grow my faith and my love for Him through the years when I felt alone and unheard so He could prepare me for something HUGE. Something I could not yet see. I thought I was ready, but God knew I was not. I learned many lessons and grew more than any period in my life that I could recall. Through the holding pattern, I allowed God to speak while I waited. Forgiveness, healing, and transformation all took place during those years. It's a time I will never regret and always recommend.

The process of protection can seem agonizingly slow at times, but understand that your Air Traffic Controller knows just the right time to release your blessing. Sometimes it may never come, and we must be okay with that.

God sees what we do not. If you are waiting on something, slow down and allow God to speak to you. When He does, do not harden your heart. If He addresses a weakness or an inconsistency in your life, don't fall apart and feel like you're a nobody or a failure. God says you're somebody! He will strengthen you. After all, He has a purpose for you.

Take these times when the holding pattern is happening in your life and work on building spiritual growth, character, and confidence. Understand that God asks us to humble ourselves during the holding pattern and trust Him more. Can you see this somehow in your life today? What are you "waiting" for? Trust Him more. He loves you, and He knows your future and every need.

"But my God will supply all your needs according to his riches in glory by Christ Jesus." (King James Version, Philippians 4:19)

He will come through for you in His time, not yours.

Day 51

HIGHER GROUND

The title of today's charge reminds me of words taken from a hymn I would sing years ago: *Lord, plant my feet on higher ground.* What does this mean to me, and how can it help my readers get energized?

I've walked through many trying seasons in my life, all of which have prepared me for where I walk now. It amazes me how God has used the elements of my storms to strengthen me for purposes I never imagined possible – purposes I would use for Him. We can all use these struggles for God's purpose in our lives if we view them correctly and reach for "higher ground".

How can I encourage you to plant your feet on this higher ground? One way is by giving God access to your soul and transforming your character – toughening up your resolve and softening your heart.

Remember that in every season of life you walk through, there will be hidden choices. In every step we take, there is the potential to bring either nourishment or poison for our life, and the choices of the two can bring us either life or death.

Many times, we step off the solid ground and plop our feet right into a mud hole. *Splat!* But why do we often seem to wallow in that filthy place, getting dirtier and dirtier?

Many times, it's because we find ourselves covered with the evidence of our old self and our past life. We feel ashamed for playing in that mud hole too long. We easily take our eyes off Jesus, and the mud-filled hole suddenly becomes deeper, swallowing us up to the point where we feel trapped and unable to climb out.

The good news is that we can climb out! It's a choice. We ask Jesus to wash away that mess of mud on our feet, up our legs, or sometimes even higher. We all have different size holes we step in. But, with Jesus, we can step into a basin of clean water, and He cleanses us. He forgives us of our sins and cleanses us from all unrighteousness as He says in 1 John 1:9.

As we climb to the higher ground, we can rest assured that from our repentance, we are clean, full of assurance, forgiven, and free.

As you move forward in your faith journey toward abundant living, you'll sometimes fall and miss the high road because of mud holes along the way. Remember that mercies await, and God is ready to forgive if we ask Him. God wants to guide your steps so that you don't plop into another mud hole along your journey of living.

With eyes focused on Him, He'll take you from where you are – providing you with nourishment, strength, and protection – and bring you to higher ground. He not only guides your steps to a better place, but He plants your feet and equips you to sustain through every step of your journey. Let it be your aim; let it be your goal.

We need to experience Christ anew every day. We need to expect the new growth in our lives and pray for it. I remember and leave you with the last phrase in the hymn *Higher Ground*. Please allow them to be your words today.

I want to scale the utmost height and catch a gleam of glory bright, but still, I'll pray till rest I've found. Lord, lead me on to higher ground.

Day 52

BROKEN TO BETTER

While our broken circumstances may not change, we can. We need to do this by clinging to scripture and discovering who God indeed is. By being willing to share our story even through the rough waters, we can look at our brokenness, see blessings coming from the situation, and believe with an intensity that God will make us better through it. It's a choice, of course. To personalize this, how you determine your outlook will prove if God will use your broken pieces of life for a better situation.

Some of the struggles and losses we face can get better. Sickness can end. Even our financial instability can become stable. Relationships can be restored, and if we walk through spiritually dark times, the bright presence of God's amazing grace can follow.

Thankfully, some of our broken times do get better, but not always!

Can you look at a circumstance of brokenness you may have or someone you know is experiencing right now? Through the storms, clinging to God and those you love and belonging to a stable church community can help you through it. No doubt you may weep oceans of tears, but God will uphold us through all the steps we take on the journey.

Faith in the furnace can bring glory to God and allow others who may be walking through losses and pain in their life to have hope. You can make a difference. Even if your situation does not change for the better, YOU can change for the better.

Embracing the better from a brokenness state means we are not ashamed to be needy. We should possess a desperate need for our Savior. The more we embrace our inability to put ourselves back together, the more we will experience the healing grace of Jesus as He remakes us into the children of God that He wants us to be.

No matter how deep we sink into the pit of our destruction, God's strong arm of redemption always reaches further. I've lived through this; therefore, I can shout it from the mountaintops. The more mistakes I've made, the longer God's arm becomes for me and the more stories of hope I can share with others.

[37]Yet even in the midst of all these things, we triumph over them all, for God has made us to be more than conquerors, and his demonstrated love is our glorious victory over everything! [38]So now I live with the confidence that there is nothing in the universe with the power to separate us from God's love. I'm convinced that his love will triumph over death, life's troubles, fallen angels, or dark rulers in the heavens. There is nothing in our present or future circumstances that can weaken his love. [39]There is no power above us or beneath us – no power that could ever be found in the universe that can distance us from God's passionate love, which is lavished upon us through our Lord Jesus, the Anointed One! (The Passion Translation, Romans 8:37-39)

We need to start taking active control over circumstances. God loves us. God wants us to cry out to Him in our time of need. Do it!

God wants us to praise Him for the times when deliverance doesn't come. Do it!

There is a way to praise God during changing circumstances. Do it!

When you need help to see God's redemptive plan through your struggles and suffering, ask Him!

All these require us to take action. After following through the proper channels of obedience, we can then celebrate the amazing example of Jesus and His righteousness and share our experiences with others. He is the one who was broken for us and makes us better no matter how hard life can get. He gives us stories to change the world. How can He use your story?

Day 53

GOD'S HEALING

As I write out these topics, trust me, prayer goes into each one. *What do I write about today, God? What will You have me learn through these writings?* My life is affected by the words God gives me each time I sit to write and help others. I have situations that arise within my heart, and God leads me through them. Oftentimes, more than not, I choose to share my writings as they bring healing not only to my life but to the lives of others, as well.

Many of us are broken in different ways – broken minds, broken hearts, broken relationships, broken lives.

God tells us we can't live close to him and not experience some healing. We all want that, don't we? It's true that we have not because we ask not. We receive the healing that flows naturally from God's presence whether you seek it or not; that's a fact. Do you realize there is so much more available to you, though, if you ask?

The first step I've found in healing is to live close to God. The closer I am to God, the more he reveals to me.

When the time is right, which is anytime we find a need for healing in our lives, God wants us to ask Him for that specific healing – healing from brokenness in us or other people, healing from disease, healing from physical or emotional damage. All of them. The healing may be quick, or it may be a process. God determines that. Our part is to trust Him and thank Him that the restoring has begun.

Nothing is more powerful than knowing we can ask God anything while we are walking in his presence.

How do we walk in his presence?

I'm going to list some things taken from Psalms 103 that may allow us to worship God and have him close to us as we walk with him in our lives.

Worship Him because:

- He forgives our sins.
- He heals all our diseases.
- He works good and justice for all the oppressed.
- He satisfies our heart's desires.
- He makes his ways known to us.
- He is compassionate.
- He is gracious.
- He is slow to anger.
- He will not accuse us.
- He doesn't harbor anger towards us forever.
- He shows great love to us who fear him with reverence.
- He doesn't treat us as our sins deserve.
- He removes our sin from us.
- He has compassion for us.
- His love is everlasting.

Praising and worshipping God is one of the most significant things we can do in our lives. It causes bondages to be broken and makes way for healing changes to begin.

Remember, the songs of worship you sing or the prayers you pray in your heart during the day will fill your soul through the night so you will have peaceful rest. It's there where healing can begin.

Read Psalm 103. The entire chapter is recommended. It praises God.

"Praise the Lord, all his works everywhere in his dominion. Praise the Lord, O my soul." (*New International Version,* Psalm 103:22)

Let's praise God and walk closely with Him throughout today and every day forward. This act of faith will bring healing into our lives.

Day 54

BEAUTY FOR ASHES

I heard this phrase but never referenced it until I felt it necessary to use in my own life. That's when I reached for it, saying, "God gave me beauty for ashes."

I've made many mistakes that I've grieved over in my life. Often, I would repeat a cycle that I thought I never would. Cycles that only continued my grieving process. To others, I may have seemed to snuff my nose at God like I didn't care. But, deep inside, oh how I did. To me, I lacked the wisdom needed to make better choices.

Through seeing my need for wisdom and praying daily for "Godly wisdom" while reciting James 1:5, God granted me that true wisdom over time, and it allowed me to make better choices. I was able to seek Him, sit with Him, grieve with Him, repent before Him, and let Him renew my life with the only wisdom I cared to possess – His wisdom. He brought to me His wisdom, which then allowed me to make better choices just as He promised me would happen. Those choices allowed me to turn those ashes of grieving and the repetition of vicious cycles into some of the most beautiful stories I could ever have imagined. My life as it has come to be.

"If any of you lacks wisdom, you should ask God, who gives generously to all without finding fault, and it will be given to you." (New International Version, James 1:5)

Do you ever look at the ashes in your life or the lives of others and feel the great sense of loss that it brings? If you do, God wants to give you the same exchange He gave me – beauty for ashes. I can tell you it works. That's how I'm able to coach others for Jesus. It's through the ashes God brought the beauty of this book.

"He has sent me...to bestow on them a crown of beauty instead of ashes, the oil of joy instead of mourning, and a garment of praise instead of a spirit of despair." (New International Version, Isaiah 61:1,3)

I can assure you that God knows what to do with any despair. Remember, seek Him first, then sit down with Him. Cast your burdens on Him, tell Him you're sorry for your mistakes, and ask Him for wisdom, which will give you a fresh mind. You'll receive beauty for ashes with all the gladness your heart can hold. I know this to be true because it has happened for me.

Day 55

TIME AND CONSISTENCY

How many of us understand that life doesn't stop moving forward? Unforeseen things happen. It's life. Because of this, we need to have money saved. To be financially healthy, this needs to be on our minds every day. Saving for a rainy day, putting your money to work, and multiplying it is the wise thing to do.

"The wise store up choice food and olive oil, but fools gulp theirs down." (*New International Version,* Proverbs 21:20)

Wow! If that isn't direct enough...

"The plans of the diligent lead to profit, as surely as haste leads to poverty." (*New International Version,* Proverbs 21:5)

A powerful key to achieving financial security are two elements: the rate of return and consistency.

It pays to start investing early, friends. When you're young, you can save small amounts and end up with much, but if you wait to begin saving, you'll need to save much more! One thing for sure, many of us cannot afford the high cost of waiting.

Many people don't have thousands of dollars to invest all at once. They must invest smaller amounts over time to build their wealth. Consistency is the fuel that makes your investments grow.

I encourage you to start investing even the tiniest amount you may have. Stay consistent, and don't take away from it. Before long, your efforts of diligence will pay off.

Day 56

SPIRIT PRAYERS

At the time when I was writing this, I had just returned from spending time in Cleveland with my stepdad who was hospitalized due to a tragic accident. My reading of God's Word during that time made me ponder the meaning of what I will call a Spirit prayer. What is a Spirit prayer, you may be asking?

When words don't come easily in our prayer life, the Word tells us, "In the same way, the Spirit helps us in our weakness. We do not know what we ought to pray for, but the Spirit himself intercedes for us through wordless groans." (*New International Version*, Romans 8:26-27)

How do you feel about this? I don't know about you, but this passage brings me great comfort. While we are consumed with our busy lives with sometimes no extra time to think straight, be consoled. God knows.

When we pray, we are talking to God. Most of us choose the words we wish to say. We want to get it just right, to be specific, to talk to God in a way that is pleasing to Him and expresses our hearts. That is a good thing, but sometimes the words don't come.

Maybe the pain is too deep, or we are confused, or the issue at hand is very complex, or the time is not there to stop and pray. Or could it be fear that holds us from prayer? We want to talk to God but don't know how to express that certain feeling at that moment. What then?

God promises when we don't have words, the Holy Spirit prays for us. He searches our hearts and knows what's going on. He pleads with God on our behalf.

When we're sad and suffering, the Holy Spirit helps us to pray.

When we are unsure about what guidance to ask for, the Holy Spirit helps us to pray.

When we are afraid and don't know where to turn, the Holy Spirit helps us to pray.

When I was overwhelmed that week in Cleveland amidst travel, heartache, and uncertainty, the Holy Spirit helped me to pray. He is still helping me as the dust settles.

When you can't find words, simply sit with God and invite the Holy Spirit to communicate with God your deepest thoughts, feelings, and fears. HE will help you. It may seem foreign to you, but God's Word is the truth. He included this statement in His Word so that we would be comforted by it.

$\mathcal{D}ay\,57$

ATONEMENT

"because on this day atonement will be made for you, to cleanse you. Then, before the Lord, you will be clean from all your sins." (*New International Version,* Leviticus 16:30)

The word "cleanse" in this verse jumped out to me. Therefore, I must write about this.

We do juice cleanses, water cleanses, detox cleanses, and nasal cleanses. But, how about a spiritual cleanse for our health?

The day of atonement, Yom Kippur, seemed to be the most important annual Holy day for ancient Jews. It was the day the high priest entered the inner chamber of the tabernacle (later referred to as the temple) to offer a sacrifice for the sins of the whole nation. The purpose of this sacrifice? To make right between God and His people.

We are God's people today. Because of the sacrifice of Jesus for our sins, every day is our day of atonement. Every day we accept that his death paid for our sins. Every day we can ask forgiveness for what may have hurt God and know that our sins will be forgiven entirely, never to be remembered again.

In reality, friends, how do we approach our God of the galaxies? In prayer with excitement? Do we approach Him with values and the love He has given us?

Do we hope that forgiveness is true and He'll forgive if we ask? We need to say TODay IS OUR Day OF ATONEMENT! This is for our health and cleansing! Can we each go to God with a heart of gratitude and thank Him that nothing stands between Him and us? My prayer for you today, friends, is that your health will benefit from atonement spoken in God's Word of Life.

Day 58

CONFIDENCE

Please pause a moment and think of someone or something that you may have placed your confidence in within the past twenty-four hours. It may be a person or a possession. Do you have it? Now, ask yourself has that person or thing remained trusted by you so far.

Confidence: a state of feeling or belief that one can rely on someone or something; firm trust. This is the description from an online dictionary I sourced.

Personally, nothing or no one has my complete confidence or trust more than God. Think for a moment where your confidence lies.

I have all the confidence I feel I need when I read God's words, which speak to my soul. It is my roadmap on the path of life, with faith for my eternal destination of heaven.

To get where we are going, we often place our confidence in other people or things. Often, we express emotion, only to be disappointed because something went wrong.

"This is the confidence we have in approaching God, that if we ask any-thing according to his will, he hears us. And if we know that he hears us,

whatever we ask, we know that we have what we asked of him." (*New International Version*, 1 John 5: 14-15)

With truth expressed in these verses, why would I trust anything or anyone else over God? This is not saying we should never trust anyone in our lives or that we shouldn't trust things that prove safe for us. It's only stating our complete confidence should rest in our heavenly Father alone to be assured of doing what He says and to be guided by Him through any situation.

If there is ever a reason one may lack confidence or be hesitant to come before God with their complete trust, we can know in these verses that He is a good God who hears our requests and cares about all our needs. We can trust in God first, placing complete confidence in Him knowing that He'll protect us. By doing so, we can be satisfied that He honors what He says, protecting our trust and confidence that we've placed in Him over all.

If what we ask for is wrong for us, He'll let us know. If it's right, He'll make it happen in His way and in His time. We can have confidence in this.

With confidence, we can trust Him enough to run into His presence just like a child who is loved and accepted by their father when they run into their arms. That's the confidence we should desire. I can't imagine receiving anything but goodness from our Father God, our Creator who loves us most.

Let's try to possess certain confidence that brings reassurance as we approach God throughout our day, that He will guarantee us a sense of safety and security that may be lacking in our lives because we are relying on other people or other things over Him.

Our overall confidence should remain in God through every situation.

Day 59

SOLITUDE

When we step away from people for a period, we have a sense of freedom. There are no expectations to live up to, no one to let down, and no one's opinions are clouding our minds. It is then that we can experience the true meaning of this word.

Solitude is spending time apart from other people.

When we pause in a true moment of silence and experience solitude, we stop making demands for ourselves and God. We can then learn we are unique, God is here with us, and that we are living in a world that is our Father's house. Experiencing this knowledge of God around us can replace the busyness, the scurrying about, and self-importance that drives so many people, including those who may consider themselves religious.

For me, it's these times when I can take off my mask, have no one around, and be myself. There is no need to talk, have answers for anyone, or even exude emotions. I can come face to face with myself and encounter God.

It's in the stillness, quietness, and peace without the presence of others that I can continue to shape my identity. We all need these growth times.

Some of us may feel anxious about being alone, while others can be alone for several hours and experience pure joy. Possibly you can experiment to discover a balance and call this a spiritual exercise for yourself to find God.

God is a friend of silence. We need silence to be able to allow God to speak to us so He can work through us.

Allow your mind to dwell on truths of the Bible regarding your true identity in God. This will help you focus your thoughts and deepen those truths that God brings to your mind. The goal is helping you learn to be more comfortable alone with yourself and God.

Nothing can separate you from God's love.

"For I am convinced that neither death, nor life, nor angels, nor rulers, nor things present, nor things to come, nor powers, nor height, nor depth, nor anything else in all creation will be able to separate us from the love of God in Christ Jesus our Lord." (New Revised Standard Version, Romans 8:38-39)

As you find a place of solitude in your day, I encourage you to try this. Allow this verse to penetrate your mind. Remember, nothing can separate you from the love of God. Say a prayer of thanks and continue about your day. Chances are you will feel refreshed and ready to see your life continued with God's presence surrounding you versus being alone.

Day 60

PROTECTION

Fear can often arise when we set out to do something in moments of faith. God often leads us to paths of healing and truth in these special times.

For me, writing in faith can be quite fearful, but writing has brought tremendous healing to my soul. As I dig deeper into God's Word for answers from my life's journey, I find more freedom knowing His love and protection surround me.

God is serious about our freedom and is protective of His investment in us.

When we refuse to deal with our fears and insecurities, we allow the enemy an opportunity to trip us up.

We need to be careful not to cover up our places of insecurities with a fake sense of life. Allow hidden lies to be uncovered and replaced with God's truth.

Jesus has no desire to expose our nakedness to a world of ridicule; He chooses to defend us. Not because we are perfect, but because we belong to Him. He loves us with great passion and protection.

"Behold, You desire truth in the inward parts, and in the hidden part You will make me to know wisdom." (New King James Version, Psalm 51:6)

Wow, God! You give us that desire not to be fearful in serving You but knowledge knowing that You will protect us as we gain wisdom and understanding in the stories You have written upon our lives.

Trust in God as your refuge. In Him lies your salvation and honor. Protection from any fear you are facing is only a prayer away. The enemy will see you as a threat but understand that God sees you as an asset. He knows where you are weak but wishes to use you in His kingdom work.

When we are at war, the victory has already been won at the cross. We can go through battles knowing we have protection by the One who saves our souls.

As you go about your day, feel the protection of the one who loves you most and who intercepts the enemy's schemes against you.

Day 61

RECONCILIATION

What does reconciliation mean? The dictionary says it's the restoration of friendly relations, the act of making one view or belief compatible with another.

I believe all of us have been through rough times where we've disagreed with someone, can't resolve our differences in a relationship, or maybe our views collide with a friend where we are in complete opposition, resulting in a broken relationship. Would I be correct? Most times, we try to make the best of it and go on trying to cover up the issue with a temporary Band-Aid, as I often say.

The words "restoration" and "compatible" makeup part of the definition of the word reconciliation. However, the root word is conciliation, which means the action of stopping someone from being angry.

God's Word teaches us that we need to make it a priority to reconcile for our spiritual health and wellness as well as others. Matthew 5:21-25 stresses to resolve disagreements as soon as possible.

We must be willing to ask for forgiveness and to forgive if we are to reconcile.

"and in one body to reconcile both of them to God through the cross, by which he put to death their hostility." (New International Version, Ephesians 2:16)

Please don't carry anger in your hearts. Your health is affected as well as the future of your life. So how do we get beyond the anger? Ask God to help you with true forgiveness.

The thing about God's POWER is in asking him. If we only wait on Him, He will dispense it on us at his will. He wants us to take our problems to Him and seek Him for what we need. Our souls find rest in Him and peace in the midst of strife. Then, when our anger is subdued, God can work.

We can pray for others at this point. We can ask God to make his presence known in their lives. We are asking Him to open their hearts so they can hear from Him. It doesn't mean there will always be an immediate response. Sometimes it can take days, weeks, months, or even years. Yes, we need to be patient.

Everything that needs to happen in our lives and the lives of others cannot happen without the POWER and presence of God. Prayer invites and ignites both.

When you want true reconciliation with a person, trust God, go to Him, and ask Him for not only your heart to change but the heart of the other person, as well. Both sides need strong prayer. We need to believe this. It's not just the other person; it's us. If this is important on your heart, you won't give up. If you feel the loss of a person and the happiness their relationship brought into your life, I encourage you to take it to God with fervent prayer, which means praying with passion and intensity! Our God knocks down barriers. Our God forgives anger. Our God heals hurts. Our God mends brokenness. Our God loves you. Our God wants reconciliation!

Day 62

REPLENISHMENT

Running myself ragged can be my "out of control" captivity in life. How can I overcome this? How can any of us defeat this way of living to accomplish something far better than we could ever imagine?

One way is to replenish ourselves with a "rest" period.

To define the word replenishment, the Collins Dictionary states it is the process by which something is made full or complete.

An example may be a cell phone and how it works.

We give our cell phones a "rest" period when the battery is running low. The phone's battery shows signs that it needs to be recharged or replenished, correct? In doing so, the machine regains full capacity of its ability to be used as an electronic device once again.

Replenishing ourselves is an important part of the forward movement in our lives. Many of us don't readily welcome rest. We are too preoccupied with our busy lifestyles to pay attention to how exhausted we may be both physically and mentally.

Our maker designs our bodies for replenishment. We exude the need to rest in the Lord and learn to trust His timing while giving Him access to who we are and who we wish to become. This all can happen in the replenishment process if we allow it.

During times of replenishment, God may reveal your true motivations, heal hidden wounds, and give you new perspectives for your future desires. He may redefine your dreams, strengthen your identity in Christ, and give you a whole new outlook on life, all while you are enjoying and experiencing your time of replenishment.

I encourage you to stop and rest throughout this day. Remember this word. Meditate on it. Every human on this planet needs replenishment.

When allowed to happen within you, you may develop a more profound sense of how much the God of the Galaxies loves you and how little you do that is apart from Him.

Remember, working on a full battery is much more effective than one that has lost its juice.

Day 63

INSPIRATION

What inspires you? Many things can inspire us deeply, but are we mindful of them? As your coach, please allow me to list some things that could be an inspiration to you as you approach your day. Try to cling to some of these biblical inspirations, which can be propelled into forward motion by allowing God's words as directive thoughts into abundant living.

"All scripture is inspired by God and is useful to teach us." (*New Living Translation,* 2 Timothy 3:16)

My prayer is that these ideas inspire you as you read them today.

1. Know where you are heading. God's word will guide your footsteps.

   "Direct my footsteps according to your word; let no sin rule over me." (*New International Version*, Psalm 119:133)

2. Have wisdom. Wisdom is one I have particularly prayed over for years, sometimes daily throughout the year.

   "If any of you lacks wisdom, he should ask God, who gives

generously to all without finding fault, and it will be given to you." (New International Version, James 1:5)

3. Find success. If you follow God's Word (Bible), life works.

   "Do not let this Book of the Law depart from your mouth; meditate on it day and night, so that you may be careful to do everything written in it. Then you will be prosperous and success-ful." (New International Version, Joshua 1:8)

4. Obey God. You need to know God and His words to be able to obey them.

   "Teach me, LORD, the way of your decrees, that I may follow it to the end. Give me understanding, so that I may keep your law and obey it with all my heart. Direct me in the path of your commands, for there I find delight." (New International Version, Psalm 119:33-35)

5. Live in purity. How can you live this lifestyle of holiness and purity without being cleansed by God's Word?

   "How can a young man keep his way pure? By guarding it accord-ing to your word." (English Standard Version, Psalm 119:9)

6. Have Joy. You can't be free of worry or unrest without God's Word in your heart.

   "The precepts of the Lord are right, giving joy to the heart. The commands of the Lord are radiant, giving light to the eyes." (New International Version, Psalm 19:8)

7. Grow your faith. We can't grow in our faith without reading God's word.

   "Consequently, faith comes from hearing the message, and the message is heard through the word about Christ." (*New International Version,* Romans 10:17)

8. You won't know what you need to be free unless you read God's Word.

   "If you hold My teaching, you are really My disciples. Then you will know the truth, and the truth will set you free." (*New International Version,* John 8:31-32)

9. Have peace. God will give to us a peace that the world can never give us, but you won't find that comfort without reading God's Word.

   "Great peace have those who love your law, and nothing can make them stumble." (*New International Version,* Psalm 119:165)

We should all be inspired to do something good today and every day. A great way to possess this inspiration of good deeds and distinguish good versus evil (since in these times everything has become so relative) is to read God's Word.

"I have hidden your word in my heart that I might not sin against you." (*New International Version,* Psalm 119:11)

Be inspired to make a change in your day by gleaning ideas from God's Word.

Day 64

GIVING GRACIOUSLY

"Wealth and honor come from you, and you are the ruler of all things. In your hands are strength and power to exalt and give strength to all. Now, our God, we give you thanks, and praise your glorious name." (New International Version, 1 Chronicles 29:12-13)

When I read this, I can't help but think of the beautiful event I was able to be a part of for our African orphans. People gave generously. I know that it was because we prayed for it to be. We met our goal. All the others who were involved stopped to pray together and remembered to give God thanks for his provisions for that event.

My husband Kenny and I gave out of our treasures and resources. We challenged others to give in the same spirit, out of honor to God. Other leaders stepped up and gave, as well. The offerings provided much funding for the building of the new safe house for our orphan teen girls in South Africa.

People were amazed at their generosity. The giving of others touched us, and we offered up praises to God for it. We exalted God and recognized him as the ultimate supplier of all things. What more appropriate way to acknowledge God as head over everything than by contributing generously to the building of a new safe house that would honor God by doing what he says in James 1:27 – care for the orphans and widows in their affliction? What better way to show trust in God's future faithfulness than to give from the abundance of his present faithfulness?

King David urged people to praise and give to God from their earthly treasures as well as giving praise to him from their whole hearts.

Powerful prayer includes extensive praise to God for his generosity. It also includes giving to God out of a praise-filled heart. To do otherwise shows that we revere our possessions more than our God who has given us all that we have.

I encourage you to give to something that God speaks to you about but to give from a healthy heart that has been blessed by God. Also, give God praise for all he will do with your generous giving. BELIEVE that He will use your giving to provide further provisions for others because He says in his Word that He will!

Maybe, possibly today, you will be able to give in a way you have never done before. Think about it, pray over it, and take a step of faith into it.

Day 65

PRAY FOR YOURSELF

I want you to know I pray before writing each of these topics.

Do you ever feel like you have no individual guidance because you're busy helping everyone else? At this point, you need to stay where you are! Concentrate on doing things each day with the presence of God being with you.

"Whatever you do, work heartily, as for the Lord and not for men."
(English Standard Version, Colossians 3:23)

Sometimes I wonder if anything I do is worth it. Then there are those days (but not many lately) where I feel it's too quiet and nothing seems to be happening. Instead of being bored by the lack of action, seek God for yourself. Sometimes it's easier to pray for others because our needs can be numerous, complicated, or even hard to determine. We are sometimes so caught up helping and praying for others that we forget about ourselves. We each need personal prayers for the day-to-day existence of ourselves. Seriously. We are often so emotionally involved in other people's lives, we forget about our own.

Do you ever feel as if your days are too busy? Do you think you're neglecting one or more areas of your life because you're trying to fill numerous roles or meet expectations others place on you? I do.

I believe we are all searching to fill a hunger for the Lord's presence in our lives. We can deeply know God, we can serve Him better, we can spend more time in prayer with Him…but how?

Just ask Him.

Pray for yourself.

God wants us to long for his presence in our lives. He wants us to walk close to him. He wants to increase our knowledge of what He says in His Word.

Pray for yourself for these things. None of this can happen by itself without prayer. You must ask God to help you become a person of a sincere, faith-filled prayer life. The Holy Spirit will teach you how to pray if you ask Him. He will help you with every aspect of your life. God will answer those prayers. Please, remember to pray for you! It's okay.

Remember, "*If you remain in me and my words remain in you, ask whatever you wish, and it will be done for you.*" (*New International Version*, John 15:7)

Wow, what a verse to close with. Thank you, God!

Day 66

FULFILLMENT

How many of us search for fulfillment daily, only to find more frustration or experience failure of being fulfilled in our lives?

One thing that prevents me from becoming frustrated over lack of fulfillment is realizing I live in a world that is imperfect. I need to voice this to myself regularly, especially while reading things on social media and interacting with others daily. There is nothing perfect in this world except God.

As your coach, I am encouraging you and others – along with myself – to continuously seek the knowledge needed to develop a close relationship with our Creator, which comes when we trust in Jesus and his words. To me, it satisfies deep yearnings and gives me joy that I can't describe.

God planted a longing for perfection in each of our hearts. It's a desire which only God can fulfill. I've been on the rollercoaster of seeking fulfillment from people, things, and even achievements, only to find myself disappointed, wanting more, or sometimes feeling a sense of loneliness attached. This desire for self-fulfillment can also become like a god or a false idol. God tells us, *"Have no other gods before Me!"*

There is a need to make God the deepest desire of my heart. Each day that I do, the peace and joy it brings to my soul far surpass any earthly fulfillment I think I want. The verse that encouraged me to write this is, "*Delight yourself also in the Lord, And He will give you the desires of your heart*". (*New King James Version,* Psalm 37:4)

May you each find fulfillment in serving Jesus and understand that He is the only one who can provide true fulfillment as you go through this day.

Day 67

OUR CALLING

I watched the movie *Letters* this past week about Mother Theresa and her life. She had a calling on her life, and no one could tell her otherwise. She was a strong woman of faith.

Many people know their calling but can't see how it will ever be realized in the details of their lives. It may be because they are trying to accomplish this in their own strength.

I don't believe God says, "Here's what I want you to do with your life. Now do it." No, this takes time. He first gives us a vision, then says He'll walk step by step with us and HE will do it through us. Remember, it's not about us. It's about God and who he created US to be. He gradually shows us one step at a time what He can do through you if you watch around you, hear His voice, and obey His truth.

Here is what I gleaned from watching Mother Theresa's story. No one could tell her otherwise what she felt God called her to do. She saw a vision and prayed through it step by step. Mother Theresa came up against obstacles that any one of us would collapse from or throw in the towel over, but she believed in her VISION from God. She couldn't accomplish it in her own strength, so she prayed daily, hourly, and continued forward. She pushed through it with beauty, love, strength, and obedience but also with kindness. I believe God protected her through each step taken and brought her life to where He created it to be with purpose. It was a beautiful story that brought peace to my soul.

If you're feeling called into something better than what you are doing at this time, let me assure you that it's probably because you are! If you have never sought God about his plans and purposes for your life, you should do that now. Better sooner than later. If you've already done so, there must be a purpose for what you are doing at this moment that you may not see. Maybe you haven't surrendered your dreams to God. In any case, know that He will not leave you where you are forever.

Try perfecting the process that prepares you to move into the calling God has on your life. I try to do this each day when I wake up and talk to God. "Lord," I say, "will you please use me however you feel you need to today?" I find myself doing things I never thought possible. It's only with God's help that I can!

"For I can do ALL things through Christ, who gives me strength." (*New Living Translation,* Philippians 4:13)

Day 68

GRATITUDE

Have an attitude of gratitude. Have you ever heard that statement? Well, there is researched neuroscience about this topic. Do you know gratitude has the power to improve our physical, mental, and emotional health? It doesn't make things feel better; it makes them get better. Truly. Giving thanks makes you happier and healthier.

If you see the world as being a mean and frustrating place, you will get that same world. If you can find any authentic reason to give thanks for anything in your life or this world, you're going to experience more joy and inner peace. People who express more gratitude are said to have fewer aches and pains, better sleep, and stronger mental clarity.

Dr. Muesli said, "If thankfulness were a drug, it would be the world's best-selling product because it has a health maintenance indication for every major organ in our system."

That was a huge statement for me.

God's Word says, *"Rejoice always, pray continually, give thanks in all circumstances."* (*New International Version,* 1 Thessalonians 5:16-18)

God knows there is a reason for gratitude. Therefore, He included it within His words of life.

Studies I've read show that an expression of gratitude leads to measurable effects on the systems of the body and brain, including:

- Mood neurotransmitters
- Reproductive hormones, such as testosterone
- Social bonding hormones (oxytocin)
- Cognitive and pleasure-related neurotransmitters (dopamine)
- Inflammatory and immune systems (cytokines)
- Stress hormones (cortisol)
- Cardiac and EEG rhythms
- Blood pressure and blood sugar

Wow!

Good fortune, changes in relationships, and more all have to do with our brain and doing what God says. Figure that. He has already solved our problems.

In good times and tough times, exercising gratitude can be one of the most powerful choices we can make.

To put into practice and build positive momentum, here are a few suggestions:

Say grace.

Take a moment to give thanks.

Keep a gratitude journal.

If you like to write, journal about the things you are grateful for or say them out loud, then pray about ten things each morning that you want to give thanks.

Share love.

Every day, tell a loved one the good you see in them. This may be difficult, especially if you don't feel you express yourself well, but each of us can try.

Always remember our mortality.

We never know how long we or anyone who we love will be alive.

Remind yourself to choose gratitude today. Be grateful for the blessings even amidst challenges that come your way. Remember, expressing gratitude makes our world a better place to live in. We each have a purpose in expressing gratitude and practicing that specific purpose brings JOY to your day.

Day 69

THANKFULNESS

Many of you may be waiting on God right now for answers to specific questions or needs. We want to know what He wants for us, but we can become impatient and want the answer now. What do we do when He doesn't answer us?

Many times, we pray the prayer again. Sometimes we try to forget the need. One of the main reasons we should pray is to give thanks for what we too often forget.

We need to remember all that God HAS done for us. We tend to ask God for more things before thanking him for what He has already given us. I find myself asking all too often, but it's just that my needs seem so great sometimes. Because of my tendency to do this, I try to make a conscientious effort to thank Him more and replace my needs with a grateful heart.

To decide to be grateful even through the tough times takes action. During times when we are sad or possibly feeling despair, this is when we need to thank Him. Yes, when everything seems to be going wrong, give Him thanks.

When our minds get snagged on a problem, ask God to show you the way to handle it. Most times, if it's on your prayer mind, you can find answers around you from God.

The very act of thanking releases your mind from a negative focus. As you turn your attention to God, your problem fades in significance and loses its power to trip you up by dwelling on it.

Many of the situations that are pounding our minds may not even be problems for today. Give these problems to God this very day so that He can deposit them into the future where He knowingly is the only One who has control over them!

Give God thanks even when you can't see the entire picture, knowing He will shed His light on your situation. We need to thank Him in all our circumstances. I believe something good always happens when we praise God. See if that proves correct in your life, as well.

We become more receptive to God's will when we pray continuously and thank him. When we do this, we allow prayer to become a natural first response to whatever is happening around us, which is healthy.

When we invite God to work in our situations, the pressure is taken off ourselves. This means, if we were leaning toward doing something that may not be what God wants for us, our hearts could be more open to what God wants, and our minds might be more willing to change.

So, when you are waiting and hoping for God to do something, continue praying and praising him with a thankful heart. Your joy will rise, and your mood will change because you realize you aren't in control anyway. God is.

A verse I would like to share with you on this beautiful day is this:

"Rejoice always, pray without ceasing, give thanks in all circumstances; for this is the will of God in Christ Jesus for you." (English Standard Version, 1 Thessalonians 5:16-18)

Day 70

TRUST

What I've learned about trust is it's not a natural response to a situation or in a person, especially for some who are deeply wounded. Some hurts can cloud our thinking and cause a stagnant life of misery if enabled.

Don't listen to the voices of accusation. They are clearly not love vibes uplifting you. If your trust has been violated in some way or another, allow the Spirit of God to take charge of your mind, sorting out those tangles of deception that have been inflicted.

God is truth. If God is living in you, be transformed by His truth that is alive within you, not the lies the enemy throws at you.

There is a song I often sing to myself. I share it with others when needed. It speaks about the voice of truth telling me a different story. When I find it hard to trust in someone or something, I revert to the inner voice inside me – God's voice of truth. It most always turns my bad story around to something positive. That voice of truth is where you receive your trust.

When no one else seems to understand you, I suggest that you draw closer to the One who understands you most, who loves you completely and perfectly. The One who created you. Confide in Him and His word for your ultimate trust in any situation you may be facing.

God wants us to put all our trust in Him in all circumstances. Try praying, asking, then going into His Word. He will equip you to get through your situation victoriously!

I've experienced this victory many times myself, and I desire it for you. I speak this because I'm living it. I still have doubts and fears, but I combat them because I have the voice of truth residing inside me. He allows me to identify where those fears and doubts come from. It is a daily battle to cast down fears and listen for the voice of truth.

Tomorrow is busy worrying about itself; don't get tangled up in that web of worry. Trust Him with one day at a time, one step at a time. Instead of trying to fight your fears, concentrate on trusting God alone. When you relate to God in trust, there is no limit to how much He can strengthen you.

By trusting in God alone, you'll find it will allow His channel of peace to flow through you. His greatest work happens when we can have a grateful, trusting heart. It's not something that happens on its own. We each must seek it with purpose!

Instead of planning and expecting, I encourage you to try trusting and thanking continuously, even if you feel uncomfortable doing it. Believe with all your heart, and it will produce a paradigm shift that will completely alter your life.

A verse my mother would always share with me through my growing years is a verse that I now claim. When challenges of life stared me in the face, my mother would say, "Trust in the Lord."

"Trust in the Lord with all your heart; do not depend on your own understanding.

Seek His will in all you do, and he will show you which path to take."
(New Living Translation, Proverbs 3:5-6)

My prayer is that God will restore TRUST inside your life as you pray over this word.

Day 71

CHOOSE WELL

Making life choices is never easy. After leaving college or a university, you must choose what happens next. Maybe you are midway through your career, facing a crossroads, and you sense that God might be calling you to something new.

Maybe you are redundant in a job you have been wedded to for years, and you are confronted by a whole new series of questions about where to go next. But, remember that the rent and bills will keep coming, so there is a degree of urgency to your situation.

Of course, such choices are usually the privilege of only a few, and we should always see it as such. However, with the speed of change in technology and the rapidly changing face of the workplace, choosing at times is frightening and overwhelming. It is almost as if we can't cope with the number of alternatives out there.

STOP!

Stay where you are, take some time out, and return to work later. Work from home or remotely, study further, change your job or possibly change the way you do it.

Maybe join in with others by doing something new, and possibly move to something more spiritual or meaningful. It may mean taking a break from full-time volunteer work or not saying yes to every person who "needs" you. The choices are dizzying.

In my experience, callings are made significantly easier by the knowledge that God is calling us out, and He's there to guide us through it. God first. That is the place to start.

The Bible makes it clear that God gives us a choice; He works with us, not just through us. For the most part, we are given the freedom to seek God's ways and then make our own choices. We do not operate independently from Him, remember this, but we aren't puppets dancing on a string either. Our callings are not commands, but beckoning and prompting. We enter into them in partnership with God, making use of the opportunities God presents to us and the passions He has given us. I believe we all have them; we just need to be quiet long enough to hear them.

Wherever you are right now (assuming that you are walking closely with the Lord and that what you are doing is neither immoral nor illegal) is where you are meant to be. Your calling is not in some elusive, otherworldly, unreachable place. Your calling is right here, right now. You are called to live in the light of the calling God has you in now. It's easy to stop and stay still, but God never told us or promised our road would be easy. He did promise never to leave us. I encourage you, my friend, stay your course. You can do it!

God has called each of us to a higher calling through Jesus. Reach for excellence with your spiritual health, physical health, mental health, and financial health. You can do it all through Jesus who strengthens you.

"I can do all things through him who gives me strength." (New International Version, Philippians 4:13)

I can believe in you, but most importantly, God believes in you. You can do this. Say it, think it, believe it, and do it with God beside you.

Day 72

HOLD OUT HOPE

It's inevitable that because life doesn't always turn out the way we imagine it will, disappointment comes at us. I often refer to my situations, disappointments, and dark times as a way to comfort others, allowing them the ability to hold out hope that their similar situation can have a great outcome for them, as well.

My ability in coaching helps not only me but also others as I work to help them understand that through these situations, the hope God has given to us all through His Word allows us to relate to one another and offer encouragement. It brings me great pleasure to see others rise above the circumstances they are facing. If I can humble myself and share it all, God has proven to me time and time again that He will honor it. My mistakes become His messages, and He showers blessings unending in the most glorifying ways that only He can do. To God be ALL the glory.

Coaching is my way of bringing hope to people by allowing them the ability to relate to another person and circumstance by creating a desire, an expectation that something good will happen if you hold out hope and not give up.

We all need hope. We should all hold out hope by placing our trust in God to heal our situations. When we depend on God, we don't rely on other people for certain things because it can be painful when they let us down. Our ultimate success or joy in life should not depend on them but God.

I speak through experiences and am sharing that God often allows hard things to happen in our lives to bless us in some way, someday, and somehow. So, hold out hope.

When disappointing things happen to you as they have for me, ask God to help you discern His truth about what you are experiencing, then hold out hope. When you experience great disappointment, do not turn bitter or be unforgiving. Run into your Father's arms so He can hold you and offer you rest as you hold out hope.

Maintain a humble, submitted, faith-filled expectant heart as you hold out hope for your situation. You will soon see God's goodness manifest during all that's happening to you. I have, and I am. When you hold out hope for your situation, our loving God will use this experience to bring you closer to Him. Trust me, your greatest story will become a treasure chest of multiple stories declaring God's presence in your life as you walked through the fire.

You can be assured that as you hold out hope for your disappointing situation, your ultimate treasure will be your deepest sense of God's presence with you through it all. Hold out hope! Don't ever give up! I'm holding out with you, and our God promises to supply everything we need while we wait!

Day 73

HELP OTHERS ACHIEVE HEALTHY LIVING

We each have friends and family who are hurting in many ways; they surround us everywhere. Usually, someone can name a hurting person quite quickly when asked. Some may be very silent about their needs, while others are almost so loud that we may tend to avoid them.

How can we be a positive influence to others?

God tells us, "*Therefore encourage one another and build each other up, just as in fact you are doing.*" (*New International Version*, 1 Thessalonians 5:11)

1. *Lead by example.* There is no better way than to be the first to do something significant. We want to help others in our family who are suffering, correct? Then we need to change first. We will capture their attention with our action, not always by the words that we speak.

2. *Make new friends.* Surround yourself with others who wish to support and affirm your healthy path of living. You can then be encouragement for them as well as them influencing you.

3. *Share your joy.* Share the Lord, new products, new stores, new ideas, and helpful information.

4. *Be bold.* People may fight against you. They aren't always saying no; they are just afraid of change. Love on them; encourage them. Don't be shy. Continue to pass encouraging words and helpful information along to them. That's what kindness is about!

5. *Pray for others.* Those who are actively trying to better themselves and those who may wish to help a loved one may need you. You may be the one placed in their life to assist them.

Another verse that describes this, *"I urge you, first of all, to pray for all people. Ask God to help them: intercede on their behalf, and give thanks for them."* (*New Living Translation,* 1 Timothy 2:1)

I believe we are all in this together, making a difference for one another for a purpose. We can make a significant impact if we allow God to use us.

Believe it.

Try to look for someone you can pour wisdom into today.

If you feel you lack wisdom, ask God for it. He won't withhold it from anyone who asks.

"If any of you lacks wisdom, you should ask God, who gives generously to all without finding fault, and it will be given to you." (*New International Version,* James 1:5)

Please reach out and help another today. Pray for wisdom, and you will get it. Then pass it along to another. God promises He will deliver it.

Day 74

PERSEVERENCE

God's Word tells us many times that perseverance, while it may not be fun, is good for us.

I'll describe perseverance as "the ability to see a problem or a situation through to its resolution despite difficulties faced along the way." It's not hard to persevere when things go your way, but when the road becomes rocky, we need strength to continue through the rough terrain.

God's Word says, "...*suffering produces perseverance; and perseverance, proven character; and proven character, hope.*" (World English Bible, Romans 5:3-4)

Hope can drive anyone a far distance, don't you agree?

In Hebrews 12:1, we are commanded to stay the course God puts us on.

"*And let us run with perseverance the race marked out for us.*" (*New International Version,* Hebrews 12:1)

We know that the enemy can try to wear us down or discourage us while we're trying to move forward. If this applies to you, ask God to help you stand firm until the enemy is defeated, whichever way he is attacking you. The enemy could be attacking your mind with doubts in your abilities to do something huge, or you could be experiencing sickness or disease in your physical body. The enemy can attack our decision to accomplish something that may reap benefits for others in the name of Jesus. Whatever it may be, ask God for strength to see you through each of the circumstances you are faced with. David never stopped until the job was finished, and neither should we. We should pray until we receive an answer.

When we persevere in prayer, it allows God's POWER to flow through us so we can withstand whatever pressures are coming our way.

Remember, with God, you can eliminate issues that come your way, and while God assists you, He gives you the perseverance to attain the result. That very result may change the world you live in. Never underestimate the POWER of God or the strength only He can give to persevere.

God is with you, and with Him arming you with strength, you will push forward. You will have the victory!

Day 75

BOLDNESS

Are you one who possesses the willingness to take risks, act innovatively with confidence and courage? If you answered yes, you might face situations ahead of you with boldness.

There are many leaders in God's Word that show us the act of boldness used within their lives.

"Jabez cried out to the God of Israel, 'Oh, that you would bless me and enlarge my territory! Let your hand be with me, and keep me from harm so that I will be free from pain.' And God granted his request." (*New International Version*, 1Chronicles 4:10)

Jabez prayed boldly, and God granted his request.

God takes pleasure in blessing us and providing for us. He wants to be with us and protect us, but He wants us to pray and ask. So often we fail to follow through. Either we feel we don't deserve His blessings, or we think we are selfish for asking, or we think we can do it alone and choose not to bother asking God at all.

If we do things with our own strength and fail to recognize God's ability to show goodness in situations, we rob ourselves of blessings that are delivered by God.

God wants to give us more than we can imagine. (Ephesians 3:20)

Praying boldly as Jabez did starts by thanking God for what He has already given you. When you do this, you can with confidence know where your goodness comes from. Then, with boldness, you can approach the throne and ask Him to bless you so that you can, in turn, bless others.

Asking in boldness is not asking too much. God won't ever give us something that isn't good for us. He won't give us something we aren't ready for either. God answers our prayers according to His will and always in His perfect timing.

When you step into life today, use boldness in a prayerful way that shows and speaks to God. State with confidence what you are asking for because you've already verbalized all that He has blessed you with up until this moment. Boldness is something that develops in us over time with practice and overcoming fear in our lives.

I encourage you to ask God to give you a sense of boldness as you communicate with Him and as you continue to develop your courage and confidence within this special alone time with God. You will soon see that God will grant your request.

Day 76

PRAISE

"Wealth and honor come from you; you are the ruler of all things. In your hands are strength and power to exalt and give strength to all. Now, our God, we give you thanks and praise your glorious name." (*New International Version*, 1 Chronicles 29:12-13)

We are challenged by King David to give. David gave his own gift out of his treasures as king. He says give in the same spirit, out of honor to God. Many of his leaders stepped up and gave, and soon had funding for the temple. People were amazed at their generosity. Touched by their giving, David offered up one of the greatest prayers of praise in the Bible. It was not a lengthy prayer, but every word exalted God and recognized Him as the supplier of all things.

After David gave his treasure and praised God, he acknowledged the profound effect he felt when the people gave their offerings. David concluded by urging the people to *"Praise the Lord your God."* (*New International Version*, 1 Chronicles 29:20) They offered to God earthly treasures as well as praised Him from their hearts.

Powerful prayers to God should always include praise as we are instructed to do. We should also give to God out of a praise-filled heart. If we don't do this, we may reveal that our possessions mean more to us than God, who has given all that we have.

Think about how you pray today. Do you tend to start your prayers with asking?

I've found by making a conscientious effort always to thank God first; it brings me much more happiness when I get to praise Him for what He has done for me. He has given me so much and is the Creator of all things I enjoy. My heart jumps with happiness as I think of the ways I can praise Him each day during my prayer times.

To a God who has given to us ALL that we have, let us PRAISE Him for everything He has done, with our hands lifted high to the heavens!

Thank you, Almighty Lord, for the abundant gifts You bestow upon us daily. We love You and praise You. To You, oh God, be ALL the glory for everything You do and everything You've done! Forever, we will praise You! We praise You! WE PRAISE YOU, FATHER GOD. Amen.

Day 77

OBEDIENCE

Some ways are right, and some ways are not. We cannot confuse the two. They become very clear, and God shows us the ways that are right when we seek Him.

God says when we seek Him, we will find Him. (Jeremiah 29:13) And when we do, He shows us the right way. At that point, we have a choice to make regarding obedience.

When we obey God, we are protected. If we obey God, He will give us the answers we need with His revelation, which allows us to get where we need to go.

When we aren't living the way He asks us to, we sacrifice many experiences that we could be enjoying in forms of blessings. Many people are not willing to exercise the obedience needed proceeding these blessings, and therefore, they rob themselves of protection, guidance, and answers to prayers. These three forms of blessings can be bestowed upon us when obedience to God is followed through.

When we obey God, we can be led by Him.

When we obey God, we see answers to our prayers.

The Bible tells us, *"receive from him anything we ask because we obey his commands and do what pleases him."* (*New Revised Standard Version,* 1 John 3:22)

There is a direct correlation between obedience and prayer.

I've come to a place where I trust Him so thoroughly that I obey whatever He says. Often, He speaks to me through His Word, and this guides me each day. Obedience isn't miserable, my friends. It becomes a privilege.

We obey because we genuinely love God and are grateful to Him for our life. By living in obedience, there will develop a strong desire to have nothing between you and God. This brings the motivation to walk in obedience to God because we won't ever wish to live in the gut-wrenching misery that comes with absence of the obedience to Him.

Ask God through prayer if there are specific steps of obedience that He wants you to take. He will tell you. Please don't start your day without prayer.

Day 78

STEADINESS

Do unexpected events throw you off course? How we respond to what comes our way can mean experiencing more peace in our lives by focusing on a mindset of consistency while pushing ahead.

Remaining calm and confident, yet consistent, can allow an easier view of the road you'll be traveling on toward your intended destination. Our view of what's ahead is important. If our mind is cloudy and cluttered, can we see what's coming ahead? Many times, not. The saying is "slow and steady wins the race." Why is that?

The definition of steadiness means "firmly fixed or placed; stable in position or equilibrium."

Steadiness is an important word for us in life. It allows you the awareness of staying planted firmly in your walk with God, not being interrupted by every "squirrel" that may jump in your way. If you're distracted, it can cause your attention to swerve, taking you off course and in another direction that you may not have anticipated.

Why is it important to remain steady?

We live in a world full of sights and sounds. We must not become a slave to these stimuli by leaping ahead of ourselves or falling behind because of any distractions. Many times, wobbling about will rob us of time to finish our task or possibly stop it altogether.

God always wants us to be aware of Him and to continue with our goals and dreams that He's placed in our hearts. It is steadiness He desires within our daily walk, moving forward with Him. Paul says, *"I press toward the mark for the prize of the high calling of God in Christ Jesus." (King James Version,* Philippians 3:14)

As soon as something grabs your attention, talk to God about it. Share your joys and problems with Him as they arise. He will help you cope with whatever is before you. Allow God to keep you steady as you make your way toward peace and accomplishing your goals throughout your day.

God will work through you when your heart is steadfast and trusting in the Lord.

Steadiness on your journey, while keeping God close to your heart, allows for a much brighter result.

"They will have no fear of bad news; their hearts are steadfast, trusting in the Lord. Their hearts are secure; they will have no fear; in the end they will look in triumph on their foes." (New International Version, Psalm 112:7-8)

Steadiness through your day will help you balance your weight and allow your Creator the ability to help you with carrying your load as well as achieving your goal.

Day 79

CULTIVATING A RELATIONSHIP

How often are we scared to death to move into new territory with Jesus? It is usually to that extent when we realize how much we need Him.

The more days, months, and years we spend with Jesus, the more time we cultivate a relationship and have adequate time to learn to trust Him.

Jesus cares about our eternal impact because how we live or don't live today resonates with us into eternity. Unfortunately, we are masking our present moment symptoms and missing the perfect opportunities of a relationship in our present midst. We can look around us at any given moment and find God in something, but that doesn't constitute a relationship with Him.

Unfortunately, when we are sick, we like to medicate. When we are afraid, we run in the opposite direction. When faced with somebody else's pain, we are quick to explain it away so that we don't have to get involved. Why is this?

God wants to involve us in the opportunities of today. He longs for us to cultivate a relationship with Him. He will help us see our abilities, show us power in our prayers, and give us possibilities where we may feel there are none.

I love the fact that God knows what we need more than we know our own needs. He pushes us to run when we need endurance. He leads us up a steep hill when we need faith muscles engaged. When we need teaching, He gives us parables. Jesus wants us to find our strength in Him so we can accomplish the impossible.

Without God's constant influence in our lives, it's all too easy to loosen our grip of faith and to trust our abilities far more.

Cultivating a relationship between you and your Savior starts by giving Him your heart. Sometimes we say things with our lips, but our actions tell a different story. (Matthew 15:8) If you desire to walk closer to the One who can carry all your baggage, grab hold of your present concerns, place yourself in the present moment, and bring all of yourself into the presence of God, allowing His power, insight, and revelation to cultivate a whole new relationship with Him.

Day 80

VIRTUE

Some of us like chocolate; some of us like vanilla. Some of us are introverts; some of us extroverts. Each of us is unique. I believe there is one thing we all have in common. Everyone wants to be happy. No one sets out to seek a dull, lifeless, boring, meaningless life. We all want to be happy all the time, and we want it for everyone we love.

Happiness is a temporary condition based on our circumstances. Many writers, including me, use the word happiness to describe "the good life", but where does it come from? What makes us happy? John Wesley said famously, "You cannot be happy without being Holy." I would agree with John; however, living in our day-to-day circumstances, we can easily be deceived.

The world's values indirectly tell us happiness comes from sex, money, and power. While television tells us that expensive luxuries will make us happy, we can see with our own eyes that well-dressed people who drive shiny, expensive cars can lead us to be happy ourselves if we mimic these situations. These are false narratives built on half-truths and outright lies. When we adopt this way of thinking, we slowly destroy our souls.

Negatively, our culture tells us not to suppress our desires, that rules are made to be broken, and nice guys finish last. Thoughts such as these can leave you sad, lonely, and capable of hurting others in your quest for happiness.

On the other hand, virtue, which is not the outward appearance but the inner reality of a heart that loves goodness, is truly beautiful.

When someone tells the truth, although it may hurt them, it's lovely to know they spoke the truth. When a man treats a woman like a person instead of an object, it's beautiful, and the action reflects it. A person who does a good deed in secret is a marvel and a wonder, leaving a warm, tender feeling.

Without virtue, there can be no happiness because virtues are the powers by which we can come to acquire happiness. A virtuous person is a light to everyone around them.

"Finally, brethren, whatever is true, whatever is honorable, whatever is right, whatever is pure, whatever is lovely, whatever is of good repute, if there is any excellence and if anything is worthy of praise, dwell on these things." (New American Standard Bible, Philippians 4:8)

I believe God tells us to dwell on these truths because by using these virtues in our lives, we can become blessings to others who are in need, allowing our lives to reflect happiness. Please think on this word "virtue" and try to incorporate this into your day-to-day living.

Day 81

KINGDOM LIVING

Patterns of living our lives on earth should start to reflect what God says in His Word about living in the kingdom of God. It's a lifestyle that will prove truth to others if we can live it out as God has directed us to do.

"For I tell you, unless your righteousness exceeds that of the scribes and Pharisees, you will never enter the kingdom of heaven." (English Standard Version, Matthew 5:20)

Pattern your inner heart after that of Jesus and not after the outer actions of Pharisees (by handwashing and Sabbath rules). Humble your hearts and work on your soul with what's most important, such as integrity, gentleness, respect, and mercy.

Let's think about this and how we can incorporate it into our lives today. What does Jesus say when he tells us "become as a child"? We know children to be innocent, trusting, and having little self-consciousness. They do not naturally judge others or hate people. Love comes naturally to them. Children do not need to be in control; they have no authority while living each day dependent on and trusting others. They receive almost everything as a gift. The Bible urges us to have this "childlike" faith. Let's transfer this to kingdom living.

Kingdom living requires submission. Submission to what, you may ask?

Kingdom living means to be born of water and spirit. First, born of water from your mother's womb just as every person on this planet was born. Then, born of the spirit, which is a second birth where you relinquish control of your life and submit to the Spirit, infusing your entire being with new life and new capacities.

This reminds me of becoming a child and learning all over again how to conduct ourselves but in a new way. When this happens, your love for God increases as does your ability to understand The Bible.

Kingdom living allows us to be indwelt by a person far greater than a set of regulations. To enter Kingdom living, we need to personally surrender our lives to the leading of the Holy Spirit. Will you allow surrender, humility, trust, and a willingness to become the kind of person who God desires us to be to take place in your body? One whose heart and character is shaped by God regardless of your past?

Let's choose Kingdom living on our journey through the life that is granted to us daily, by God. Live and remember the "childlike" faith that Jesus talks to us about in Matthew 18:2, and bring this back to Kingdom Living.

Day 82

HOSPITALITY

When we speak of hospitality, we are often addressing issues of inclusion or exclusion. We each make choices about who will and will not be included in our lives. God cares deeply about those who are left out. Our entire culture excludes many people.

Not always am I comfortable in group events, and many times, I would choose to be home alone over entertaining people or attending a social gathering. Unfortunately, in the lifestyle my husband and I wish to live, people are a huge part of our life. Therefore, we don't always have the option to spend time alone. Practicing hospitality is asked of us by our Lord. Showing hospitality to our neighbor can at times make us vulnerable, and we opt for ways to ignore doing it.

How can I make room? Room in my heart, on my calendar, and in my home? How can you make room?

There are always people for whom we should make room. The new neighbors moving in across the street, the one who's a liberal while you're a conservative, the couple who stepped in front of you while waiting in line at the football game, spending time in a life group under a tiki hut as we do. The list goes on, but before any of this, can we make room for our Lord who promises us His presence whether or not we take the time to be present with Him?

Living in God's kingdom involves loving God and loving others, too. We need to invite others and include others, which reflects our King, our Savior, a God of hospitality.

Let's think of ways others may have been hospitable to us. Did they offer their time to you? Has anyone ever made a meal for you so you could be freed from preparing it? Has anyone ever offered a space for you to sit down if you were the only one left standing?

Even more extravagant than the hospitality offered to you by others, think of what is provided to you by the Father Himself. I was an orphan; He called me His daughter. I was a foreigner; He made me a citizen. My sin made me unclean like a leper; He didn't cast me out.

Hospitality is often unkept and almost always inconvenient. Making room is not about our comfort. It's taking something you think is yours and offering it to someone else.

Jesus made room for all types of people, neighbors, the poor, His betrayers, strangers, children, and many more. He gave of Himself, offering Himself to others and the Father.

Making room is a selfless act. It's taking the focus off you and placing it on someone else despite their need, want, or situation. Can we remember today to be hospitable to others and make room?

"We love because He first loved us." (English Standard Version, 1 John 4:19)

Sharing with the Lord's people who need your time, or being a good listener, or doing small things to show you care about other people will allow you to practice the word hospitality and put it into action today.

Day 83

DELIGHT IN TREASURE

As a child, I remember desperately searching for lost treasure. In my mind, the treasure resembled beautiful, shiny jewels of various colors that I might find hidden within an old treasure box buried in the dirt somewhere or alongside a riverbed. I always believed I would find this treasure. Listening to the fables of my parents and grandparents, they would play their fun and trickery on me as a child by sometimes planting a clue. They would lead me on paths to hunt for such things that never existed. But, in my mind, these jewels were real – a treasure I painted a picture of for a lifetime.

When we humbly bow before God, He gives us treasures. He also allows us to carry His treasures, things that are dear to Him – His glory, His power, His Holy Spirit, and His message to a lost and dying world despite knowing very well we could make mistakes, take the credit, or completely miss the mark with them. God knows how imperfect and selfish we can be. Still, He entrusts us with His treasures because He loves us.

God surrounds us with desirable treasures, leading us on paths of grace, mercy, and providing all the supernatural help we can ever need to find it. He leads us on the path to eternal treasures that come by allowing us to join Him in His kingdom work. What an honor!

What a reward He gives us for having the faith and courage to step up and work beside Him. He makes our heart His home if we allow Him inside to live with us.

God will reveal His wisdom and love to you through refining moments just as He has done for me. I've learned this many times over and prayed for His treasure of wisdom, which He speaks of in James 1:5.

"If any of you lacks wisdom, you should ask God, who gives generously to all without finding fault, and it will be given to you." (New International Version, James 1:5)

I've found that my greatest delight is in mining my treasure of Godly wisdom. In the creative process of spiritual truths, I've learned I can encourage, strengthen, and nourish others while coaching my audience to their delights in treasures.

I shudder to think of the treasures I would have missed out on if I never prayed and asked for the Godly wisdom I've received. I humbled myself to Him, and He poured out His treasures on me generously without finding fault, just as He said He would do.

Delight yourself in God's treasures today. He will give you the desires of your heart.

"Delight yourself in the Lord, and he shall give you the desires of your heart." (New King James Version, Psalm 37:4)

Day 84

IMPERFECTION AND PERFORMANCE

One of the beautiful things about following a shepherd is He's always with us. He doesn't base His care for us on how perfect we are or how well we perform in front of others.

Lord, you would leave the ninety-nine and go after that one lost sheep despite its imperfections and performance. I heard my friend pray this prayer. I thought about this vivid picture in my mind and understood it to be the truth. Yes, God would do this.

God is always stirring within us a desire to know Him more. He's creating in us a hunger for His Word. We grow with God as we walk with God and follow His lead, just as the sheep grow while following their shepherd and hearing their voice. But, what if one single sheep wandered off the path? Not because of imperfections in its body or performance in the herd, but because it simply got lost. Is it right that the shepherd would leave his ninety-nine? Many of us think that's an awful lot to leave unattended, but what if that one sheep was you?

God says you are worth it. Your value means everything to Him that He would leave the ninety-nine to come after you.

As you give yourself to God's special assignment, you will pray more and grow with a more profound sense of passion. You will realize you have value in God's eyes. You are constantly being guarded by God, assuring you that you will safely arrive in heaven. When something takes you down another path, be sure the shepherd who loves you and forgives you is eagerly searching for your safety. Read about it in Luke 15:4.

He hides your imperfections and performance in the cleft of the rock, along with mine, and covers us there with His hand. He protects our life with the depths of His love and the perfection of salvation along with His incredible act of love, allowing each of us to take great comfort, stability, and consistency into our lives. Despite the mess-ups of our performances or the lack of consistency in our imperfections, we need to recognize our value to Jesus. God doesn't see those things; He sees our heart to please Him. Don't be distracted. Instead, be encouraged that He will always come after you despite how you feel about yourself.

Day 85

CONTENTMENT

How can we understand contentment and put it to use in our lives for today and more abundant living in the future? Apostle Paul told Timothy, *"Now godliness with contentment is a great gain."* This is a POWERFUL exhortation, but let's look at the word contentment for what it is. It is a state of happiness and satisfaction.

The freedom of simplicity and joy of contentment lead us to a Kingdom living solution, which is not stinginess or carelessness but rather a simplicity. Simplicity is something easy, plain, natural, and it's easy to understand. It's an inner attitude that can affect what we choose. For example, when it comes to a purchase, the freedom that simplicity offers can bring on the joy of contentment. Let's dive in a little deeper.

How would you rate yourself in the area of simplicity in your day-to-day living? Can you make simplicity an inner reality and not a law, if you so choose? Yes, you can, and by doing so, you can also adapt the right perspective when it comes to wealth, knowing that it's a provision from God and must not be treated as a god.

It is important to have the inward reality in place so we can make our outward lifestyle decisions, and then these decisions can help us with contentment. There are many choices one can make. Take shopping for instance. When it comes to our purchases, we are faced with having to decide what we want versus what we need. Some questions you can ask yourself about simplicity might be, *Do I really need this or will my money be better spent on something else? Even better, should I invest my money in a heavenly treasure?*

In an "abundant living" lifestyle, there are ways to use our money. The apostle Paul does not say money is the root of all evil. He said the "love" of money is the root of all evil.

We need to be careful not to become ensnared with loving money. When we want to make purchases, we need money to do so. However, sometimes those purchases can become desires and may take us to uncontrolled situations in our life. Those uncontrolled situations may bring on desires in us, adopting the "love" of money which Paul speaks of in 1 Timothy.

Paul reminds us, "*...there is great gain in godliness combined with contentment; for we brought nothing into the world, so that we can take nothing out of it; but, if we have food and clothing, we will be content with these. But those who want to be rich fall into temptation and are trapped by many senseless and harmful desires that plunge people into ruin and destruction. For the love of money is a root of all kinds of evil, and in their eagerness to be rich some have wandered away from the faith and pierced themselves with many pains.*" (*New Revised Standard Version,* 1 Timothy 6:6-10)

Contentment in abundant living within God's kingdom requires wisdom. I, personally, pray for this type of wisdom daily – Godly wisdom as James 1:5 describes. We need to examine the ways we spend money, how we think about possessions, and how we view them in our lives.

Today, being a steward of God's money, I'm less likely to spend it on frivolous things I don't need. I may still make that mistake, but I quickly acknowledge it and try to do better next time. I am a child of God living in His abundant kingdom and not under law. By viewing it this way, it allows me the freedom to make a choice, but this is where I ask God for His wisdom to make *right* choices.

I'm learning Godliness with contentment is a great gain, and there are days when I ask the questions:

- Do I need this?

- Will it bring me joy in God's kingdom or temporary happiness?

As I journey through life, I'm praying consistently to find more contentment in "giving" to serve Jesus than in "buying" to please myself. It's a personal choice, but I know God will bring me peace if I ask for His guidance when making choices, especially in my purchases.

I desire and strive for godliness with contentment, which God speaks about in His Word. This is what I believe brings on true inner peace and an abundant living lifestyle. I'm trying to simplify in many areas of my life currently, and I try to remember to pray before making any major purchases. It's something I am learning.

If you feel you need more contentment in your daily living, try praying that God reveals it to you while making decisions you are faced with in your life. If we wish to possess an abundant living lifestyle, we need to learn to be content with what God has provided for us. Praying over everything with a grateful heart helps. Remember, godliness with contentment is a great gain.

Day 86

WONDERFUL WORSHIP

Learning to glow in a time of worship can be life-changing. I'm so different these days because of learning how to worship my Savior wonderfully.

It's not enough that you should read about worship, hear worship songs, or listen to others as they worship. You must worship God with a heart full of love for Him. Step out in faith and purposely tell God that you want to worship Him!

In your worship times is where you will develop an intimate relationship with God. If you don't feel that intimacy while you are worshipping by yourself, continue to praise and worship Him until you do. It's not that you must try hard to get close to God; He has chosen to be close to you in your praise.

Our souls need to have barriers broken down and walls penetrated so our hearts can be wide open for God to pour Himself into us. Worship is a special time between you and God to do this.

When you look for the beautiful worship moment, God must be your complete focus. Put all other distractions out of your mind. At that moment, you will sense why God created you. You will hear

God speak to your heart because your heart softens the closer you come to His presence. He changes your emotions, attitude, and the way you think.

During my worship with God, He pours out His Spirit on me, clears my mind to focus on Him more, and breathes life back into me. I feel refreshed, renewed, and free in wonderful worship time with my Savior.

If you are feeling empty, allow Him to fill you even today. Let Him infuse you with His power and joy. Stay in a worship state and let God take away all your fear and doubt. He can break chains that imprison you and restore you to a whole new presence in Him. Fall on your face in front of God and watch how He will lift you above your circumstances and limitations. It's the best place to be, to feel freedom and love from your King.

I think of a time where I just came back indoors from running. I put on worship music and began doing floor exercises. I soon decided to stop with my exercising and get in the moment with God. I wanted to focus on worshipping Him completely. I turned face down on my mat, stretched out my arms, and praised God at that moment. Glorious emotions took over my body. I cried out to Him in wonderful worship while face down on the floor and with no distractions! I felt so full of love from God my Savior. Those twenty minutes of intense worship cleansed me thoroughly.

I love how God revealed to me through that wonderful worship moment that not only does He give me wings to fly, He also motivates me to help others find life in Him. He exhilarated me in such a short time because I stayed in that moment of connection with Him.

As I coach you to this place of intimacy with God, I encourage you to stay there long enough to complete your time of focus on Him. Wonderful worship in God's presence will lift your spirit to new heights of freedom and restore wholeness where you were once empty. Pause long enough to allow yourself the precious time needed for wonderful worship in your day or week.

Day 87

PASSION FOR PRESENCE

Just being with God fills us with joy, but taking the next step in developing a passion for His presence allows you to experience the joy of the Lord in the midst of any situation because it's found in His presence.

To be in God's presence here on earth doesn't mean people will never die and everyone will be healed, or that our prayers will always get answered. It means if we develop a passion for being in His presence, we know He will never leave us or forsake us no matter what happens. He tells us this in His Word. (Hebrews 13:5, Deuteronomy 31:6) He will always be everything He is. We can have joy because of His presence, even when we pass from earth to be with Him in heaven forever.

I have witnessed people dying, and I've heard stories about people's "last breaths" that would confirm some of them left this earth having possessed "true passion for God's presence" in their last moment of life. The joy and peace that comes over not only their faces and bodies, but that which encompasses their souls and entire being, comes to them because of the passion in their hearts to finally see Jesus face to face. It is an overwhelming sight. I believe most of these people learned that God's presence is addicting, and they longed to see Him in person at this point versus the Spirit they have known prior.

I believe God's ultimate goal is to get us to know Him while we are living. We can't know Him fully unless we spend time with Him in the stillness, in His presence. We need also to allow Him to "be" in ours. We need to rest in His holy presence.

Will you let go of everything and just "be" with God so you can worship Him for who He is? You can start developing a passion for God's presence by the joy and rest you experience while in this place. The more we can experience the true presence of God in our daily lives, the more we want of Him. It's a beautiful underlying feeling that everything is going to be ultimately good.

I encourage you if you've ever been passionate about anything, reflect on it and what your feelings were that came from the passion you possessed. I assure you that nothing can EVER compare to the passion of God's presence once you've experienced it.

May you learn and develop this joy from a source that never runs dry and becomes your strength. My life is changed because of my passion for His presence.

"Blessed are those who have learned to acclaim you, who walk in the light of your presence, Lord." (New International Version, Psalm 89:15)

Living an abundant life would not be complete without possessing a passion for presence and the full benefits of experiencing this. May we each develop the passion of presence that brings such joy – His presence.

Day 88

BEST PLANS EVER

We each have plans and dreams for our lives. We think we know what's best and if God just followed our plan, everything would be perfect. But God's plans are much bigger than ours.

By trusting that God is for us and not against us, we can see our future as He sees it.

God has a future filled with plans to prosper you and not harm you. Jeremiah 29:11 explains that He wants to give you hope and a future. He wants to bring you closer to Him.

Sometimes in life, we might be holding on to things very tightly, but God may be calling you to let go of them, leave them behind. Why you ask? Because He wants you to take hold of a greater blessing.

When I was younger, I dreamed of what a perfect life would look like for me. I pictured my future and imagined my life today, but it was entirely different than I thought it to be.

When you were a child, what did you think you would be when you grew up? Has God led you toward or away from that childhood sense of what your future would hold?

If we think about it, Abraham's faith journey had its highs and lows. He believed God's promises from a young age. Yet, he got out into the real world and struggled to trust those promises because he went through some hard times. We can relate to that story when it comes to the growth and plans within our own life.

God has a plan for your life. The plan is about the journey, the process, and the relationship of faith that's built with every shaky step you take.

We need to believe that the very God who loves us – and loved us enough to give us his only Son – has a far greater plan for our lives than we could ever dream up. When we let go of this world is when we can find God's best plans for us.

Hold tightly to what I say to you today in the fact that when you place your trust in the One who vows never to let go, you don't ever have to have a bad plan. With strength, humility, and inviting God to surprise you with a new direction in life, you can align with His will, even if it doesn't line up with yours. Then you will have the best plan ever!

Day 89

HEAVEN

I'm thankful for the quiet days, although I don't seem to experience them as much as I once used to. When I get bored by the lack of activity in my life, I often use this routine to seek God's face. As I do, I grow closer to Him. In these times, I reflect on heaven, which is both present and future.

To me, these times could be the glistening sunshine that awakens my heart as I glance out my window, or the birds chirping, or the colors of the trees and skies. When I see and hear these, I sing praises to God or pray and thank Him!

You can find glimpses of heaven along your path when you keep your eyes and ears fully open to God.

When we reach the end of our life-path, there is an entrance to heaven. Only God knows when you will reach that destination, but please know He is preparing you for it each step of the way.

I am convinced that each of us will reach our heavenly home in God's perfect timing. It won't be a moment too soon or a day too late, my friends.

As you walk along life's journey, I encourage you to walk it in healthy thoughts, actions, and of course, along the path of life with God. The hope of heaven will encourage you more the closer your walk is with our Savior.

"We have this hope as an anchor for the soul, firm and secure. It enters the inner sanctuary behind the curtain, where our forerunner, Jesus, has entered on our behalf." (*New International Version,* Hebrews 6:19-20)

I find it a pure pleasure to think of heaven and what's awaiting those who earnestly seek our Savior.

God says, *"If you seek me, you will find me."* I encourage you to find the One who loves you most, your Creator, and in doing so, you will see a glimpse of heaven.

Day 90

FUEL FOR LIFE

How can we better connect with God? We all have busy days, but what allows us that true inner peace with God is a deeper relationship by knowing Him.

Through coaching and accountability, I have developed a pattern, or a routine so to speak, which I have happily shared with others through the years to strengthen their relationships with God. This effort to develop consistency has allowed me a deeper, stronger walk with my Savior each day. To simplify this, I've written it out for you to try. I encourage you to walk out these highlighted steps for a week and see what depths of connection follow to align you with our Savior and allow you the life of abundant living.

1. Get plenty of rest and wake up early each day. Let your first thoughts of the morning be on God. It's an act of honor and respect for who He is. Have a thankful heart from the moment you open your eyes. Be thankful you are still alive. Dwell on your thankfulness to God!

2. When you are ready for the day, allow a half hour of quiet time devotion to God. Submit to Him. Allow Him entrance into your life each morning before the day starts. Make the

time. If you need to, set the alarm to wake up earlier so you can do this. It's God's time; it doesn't belong to you.

3. Read the Word daily or some spiritual guidance material that will allow you to apply what you've learned when times get tough while living.

4. Fuel your day with the reflections of what you read that morning. Don't let it leave your mind throughout the day. Turn your mind inwardly where you will find God. We all have our own "places to find Him." You will have to make an effort until it becomes a routine. None of us are too busy for God, right?

5. Pray. Set those conscientious times to speak to God throughout your day. Try not to have them be routine, like right before you eat or just before you go to bed. Talk to Him through the duration of each day. Include Him. Don't just talk in your mind; speak out loud when you're alone or in the car driving. It's amazing to me how well I can communicate with God when I talk out loud to Him. I focus better. He wants to hear from you. He wants communion with your soul.

6. Remember, as you prepare to sleep, your ending thoughts before you close your eyes should always reflect God. Give Him your thoughts about the day. Also, remember to examine yourself before God. This is very important and needs to be done regularly to keep the communication open between the two of you. Seek His wisdom and turn whatever issue you may have over to Him. Even if you're unsure if it is a sin or not, turn it over to Him. Release it. Confess it. Make a resolution with God to improve your tomorrows. Bask in

God's peace as you close your eyes and rest. You will notice a difference in your restful sleep, and it will increase for you as you continue to keep all your thoughts focused on God during the night.

My husband and I have tried to follow this pattern individually throughout our married life, and often, if not almost daily, we join together on many of these steps. This will keep your marriage closely knitted by allowing God to reign over both of you together as one heart before God.

As you sleep and when you rise, God will bless your heart and entwine it with His whether you're single or married. Connection with Him is our Fuel for Life.

Afterword

YOU DID IT! Congratulations on completing your 90-day coaching guide to an abundant living lifestyle.

My prayer is that you've been deeply connected to the awareness of the presence of God in your life. If you've strengthened your faith and broadened your desire to impact the world in a powerful way, that is important to me, but most of all, it's important to the God you serve. If you've journeyed through the past ninety days of coaching with reassurance, comfort, and hope from God's Word, you will be experiencing a taste of the abundant living lifestyle God intended for you.

God tells us in Ephesians 3:20 to never doubt God's mighty power to work in you and accomplish all this. He will achieve infinitely more than your greatest request and most unbelievable dream and exceed your wildest imagination! He will outdo them all, for His miraculous power continually energizes you.

This verse is motivating. The truth of the content comes alive when you step out in faith.

As you reflect on the past ninety days of content with a new routine of challenges, I encourage you to go back and re-read them once more, but this time with a deeper understanding of what God can do through these "charges" of life. As you hold tight to the scripture verse Ephesians 3:20, place its words before you each day as you read, knowing God has every intention of using you, His magnificent masterpiece, to accomplish infinitely more than your wildest imagination.

Abundant living comes alive when you are confident God is using you. When you are a vessel that is used by the living God to accomplish your greatest purpose in which He created you to do, abundant living dwells in you.

My continuous prayer over *Fuel for Life* is that any time you reflect over the daily topics in this book, you will be inspired to achieve abundant living throughout your lifetime here on Earth and that God will quicken your heart with His miraculous power, energizing you to achieve your most unbelievable dream beyond your wildest imagination!

Fuel Your Life into abundant living.

Made in the USA
Columbia, SC
15 May 2019